Health Literacy from A to Z Practical Ways to Communicate Your Health Message

Helen Osborne, MEd, OTR/L

Health Literacy Consulting

Natick, MA

JONES AND BARTLETT PUBLISHERS

Sudbury, Massachusetts

BOSTON   TORONTO   LONDON   SINGAPORE

World Headquarters

Jones and Bartlett
Publishers
40 Tall Pine Drive
Sudbury, MA 01776
info@jbpub.com
www.jbpub.com

Jones and Bartlett
Publishers Canada
2406 Nikanna Road
Mississauga, ON L5C 2W6
CANADA

Jones and Bartlett
Publishers International
Barb House, Barb Mews
London W6 7PA
UK

Library of Congress Cataloging-in-Publication Data

Osborne, Helen, 1948-
    Health literacy from A to Z : practical ways to communicate your health / Helen Osborne.
        p. cm.
Includes bibliographical references and index.
ISBN 0-7637-4550-2 (pbk.)
    1. Health education. 2. Communication in medicine. I. Title.
RA440.O825 2004
613'.071—dc22

                                                                    2004007882

Production Credits
Executive Editor: Jack Bruggeman
Production Manager: Amy Rose
Associate Production Editor: Tracey Chapman
Editorial Assistant: Kylah McNeill
Marketing Manager: Ed McKenna
Manufacturing Buyer: Amy Bacus
Cover Design: Kristin E. Ohlin
Composition: Northeast Compositors
Art: AncoArt
Printing and Binding: Malloy, Inc.
Cover Printing: Malloy, Inc.

Printed in the United States of America

08 07 06 05   10 9 8 7 6 5 4 3 2

To Frank, Eric, and Hilary ~
for listening, laughing, and being logical

Contents

Health Literacy from A to Z

Health Literacy from A to Z

Contents

The practice of medicine has shifted from what health providers do *to* patients to what health providers do *with* patients. Health providers may recommend and prescribe treatments, but 50% of the time patients do not follow them. Furthermore, patients, by practicing better health behaviors such as not smoking, following a low-fat diet, and exercising, could do more for their health than by taking drugs or undergoing procedures. The written word is critical for clinicians to work effectively *with* patients to promote better adherence and to change health behaviors.

But health providers face two problems. The first is recognizing when patients do not understand written words; the second is knowing how to communicate through words, pictures, computer screens, and other visual media.

Helen Osborne's book *Health Literacy from A to Z: Practical Ways to Communicate Your Health Message* includes strategies to help health providers cope with these problems. Demonstrating a sophisticated knowledge of medicine and healthcare, Helen shows sensitivity to the communication problems that health providers— of all levels and disciplines—face everyday. From "A to Z," she provides a myriad of remedies that we, as clinicians, can use to recognize and overcome the barriers that prevent us from using health education materials more effectively. As a clinician educator who has been practicing and teaching primary care medicine for more than 30 years, I found this book to be a ground-breaking text. Not only did I find it enjoyable to read, but also a valuable resource for effectively using the computer and Internet, which have given patients the opportunity to become more involved with their health providers. This book greatly enhances the importance of health communication at a critical moment when health providers are feeling overwhelmed by the demand for their services. This book highlights ways providers can use health educational materials to help patients to take more responsibility for their own care.

Samuel M. Putnam, MD, MPH
Associate Clinical Professor of Medicine, Boston University
Staff Physician, East Boston Neighborhood Health Center
Co-Founder, American Academy on Physician and Patient

Editor and author of publications on teaching and research in medical interviewing, including Lipkin, M., Lazare, A., Putnam, S. M., *The Medical Interview: Clinical Care, Education and Research*, Springer Verlag, New York, 1995.

Health literacy matters. Perhaps you educate patients about illness, treatment, and care. Maybe you communicate with the general public about wellness, prevention, and early detection. Or you may be a patient, caregiver, or family member who must understand a new diagnosis or self-care instruction. Or, perhaps, as a community member and neighbor, you want to help others lead healthier lives.

Regardless of your perspective, you know the value of understandable health communication. You notice that a person with limited literacy skills is better able to follow self-care instructions when the teaching sheets are easy-to-read. You see someone from another country beam with understanding when you draw pictures instead of just talk. And your neighbor says how much she or he appreciates your suggestion to visit the local consumer health library. These are all examples of health literacy in action.

Health Literacy from A to Z: Practical Ways to Communicate Your Health Message is about all the ways we communicate health information. Whether you are a health provider, public health specialist, health educator, practice manager, literacy teacher, professor, student, scientist, librarian, patient, or family member, this book is for you.

Thank you for joining with me to make healthcare more understandable.

~Helen Osborne, MEd, OTR/L

Acknowledgments

Health literacy is bigger than any one person, profession, or program. We share the problems of misunderstanding. We also share responsibility for communicating in ways other people can understand.

This book would not be possible without the help of many people who graciously shared their stories, resources, opinions, and expertise. From A to Y, my most sincere gratitude and appreciation goes to:

Debi Arsenault, Ayako Barnum, Carolyn Bottum, Kevin Brooks, Jack Bruggeman, Pat Campbell, Linda Caraway, Dorothy Carey, Ken Crannell, Mary Ann Djonney, Russell Dollinger, Shanna Duncan, Julian Evetts, Valerie Fletcher, Ellen Fulton, Herb Fulton, Ediss Gandelman, Michel Gauthier, Sarah Goldammer, Andrea Gwosdow, Mark Hochhauser, Julie Hodorowski, Peter Houts, Marie Ivnik, Karen Jacobs, Naomi Karten, Thomas Kidder, Eric Kingson, Kathy Kosednar, Gary Kreps, Linda Johnston Lloyd, Martha Merson, Jeanne McGee, Annette O'Connor, Suzanne O'Connor, Lisa Pacitto, Lorna Patrick, Tania Phocas, Rexann Pickering, Taryn Pittman, Colleen Potter, Samuel Putnam, Yadira Ramos, Terry Ruhl, Daniel Z. Sands, Marisa Scala-Foley, Carol Schlef, Mary Jane Schmitt, Marge Schneider, Mary Schutten, Frank Sespico, Julia Stock, Mark Tatro, Linda Varone, Archie Willard, and Debbie Yoho.

Thank you!

Health Literacy from A to Z: Practical Ways to Communicate Your Health Message is written for busy health professionals and people like you who want to learn more about effectively communicating healthcare information. Designed as an easy-to-use reference guide, this book includes ideas you can use on communication topics you struggle with, are curious about, or want to learn and use.

This book is written in a way to inform you, not overwhelm you. Content is presented somewhat informally, as if you and I were having a conversation. While the book includes plenty of ideas, examples, and resources on many topics, each section stands alone. This means that if you're rushed today, you can quickly find the information you need now. Tomorrow, when you have extra time, you can read more.

This book brings together the shared wisdom of many people. I've drawn from more than 200 resources including books, peer-reviewed journal articles, brochures, papers, and websites of national and local organizations. I also build on my two other books as well as the 60+ articles I've written as a columnist for the *Boston Globe's On Call* magazine. In addition, I interviewed an untold number of people who graciously shared their healthcare experiences. Their quotes, stories, examples, and suggestions are scattered throughout.

Arranged alphabetically from A to Z, the topics in this book cover a wide variety of strategies to communicate health messages. Each topic begins with "Starting Points" of general information, often accompanied by a story or example. "Strategies, Ideas, and Suggestions" focuses on issues to consider and specific actions you can take. Please keep in mind that these are intended only as a starting place—you will need to choose the strategies that are right for you and for your work setting. "Sources to Learn More" has a wealth of print and web links I used in my research and think you might find equally helpful.

Because I assume that the primary audience for this book is health providers—those from any discipline who have responsibility for patient care—most of the examples take place in clinical settings. But even if you are not a health provider, this information can also apply. Just take the information that is relevant and adapt it to your setting, substituting words and examples that have more meaning for you. Here are some interchangeable words and terms:

- Providers, health professionals, clinicians, health educators, medical writers, graphic designers, librarians, teachers
- Patients, families, caregivers, clients, readers, library users, web visitors, students
- Appointments, meetings, encounters, interactions, home visits, classes
- Offices, clinics, hospitals, medical facilities, community centers, schools

You may notice common themes in various sections and topics. For example, plain language is often mentioned as a useful strategy. Technology, too, shows up in several places such as touchscreens, email, and web design. And sometimes methods are so important that they are mentioned more than once, like the importance of knowing your audience or confirming understanding. You can find a summary of these themes in the quick reference sheet, "Eight Ways You Can Improve Health Communication."

Health Literacy from A to Z: Practical Ways to Communicate Your Health Message is not intended to just be read and put back on the bookshelf. Instead, it is designed as a tool of action. Write notes in the book's margins or highlight and circle strategies you want to try. Share examples and stories with your colleagues and talk about how these situations relate to your setting. Go online or to the library and research the topics that interest you the most. Then use the ideas and strategies that make sense for you and the people you are communicating with. That's what this book is all about.

Now it's up to you.

About Health Literacy

Starting Points

Health literacy is about communication and understanding. It affects how people understand wellness and illness, participate in health promotion and prevention activities, weigh decisions about treatment, take medications, and follow self-care instructions. Indeed, health literacy is essential throughout the entire continuum of care.

Because health literacy includes the word "literacy," many people assume that it is only a concern for those who cannot read; this assumption is incorrect. People have difficulty understanding health information for a range of reasons including literacy, age, disability, language, culture, and emotion. I know. Although I am a health professional with many years of education, when a provider tells me upsetting news I tend to "shut down." For at least a little while, I cannot truly comprehend what my health provider is saying or asking me to read.

Health literacy is also about the many ways that providers communicate with patients, their families, and caregivers. It is so much more than just one-to-one conversations or printed pamphlets. Indeed, health literacy is a factor in all forms of health communication—telephone conversations, email messages, pictographs, websites, groups and classes, touchscreen technology, hands-on objects, and a myriad of other methods. Regardless of its form, the goal of this communication is always to promote understanding.

Experts have yet to agree on a single definition of health literacy. Some say that health literacy is about specific skills that patients need. Others say that health literacy is a continuum of tasks that extends beyond medical settings. Here are some commonly-used and well-regarded definitions:

- "Health literacy is the degree to which individuals have the capacity to obtain, process, and understand basic health information and services needed to make appropriate health decisions." From *Healthy People 2010*, a U.S. public health initiative.

- "Health literacy is a constelllation of skills, including the ability to perform basic reading and numerical tasks required to function in the health care environment." From the *Ad Hoc Committee on Health Literacy for the Council on Scientific Affairs, American Medical Association.*.

- "Health literacy has three levels: functional health literacy, which refers to communication of information; interactive health literacy, about the development of personal skills; and critical health literacy, needed for personal and community empowerment." From *Nutbeam*, 2000.

While I support and agree with all these definitions, to me health literacy goes beyond the individual. My working definition is that "health literacy is a shared responsibility in which patients and providers each must communicate in ways the other can understand."

Figure 1.1 Health Literacy—When Patients and Providers Truly Understand One Another *Source:* Mark Tatro, Rotate Graphics

Strategies, Ideas, and Suggestions

Health literacy is a worldwide concern. As stated by the World Health Organization, "Improved health literacy is necessary for people to increase control over their health and for better management of disease and risk. Communications strategies that increase access to information and build the capacity to use it can improve health literacy, decision-making, risk perception and assessment, and lead to informed action of individuals, communities, and organizations" (World Health Organization, 2001).

Why health literacy is important now. Health literacy has only recently come to the forefront as an important healthcare issue. I see several reasons for this timing. In part, patients need to quickly understand health information because they have less face-to-face time with their providers, whether in outpatient settings or during hospitalizations. Also, patients now must weigh the value of the medical and health content they find on the Internet. Additionally, people must be able to advocate for themselves as they are increasingly seen as active consumers rather than passive recipients of treatment and care.

Cynically, I also think that health literacy is an important issue today because the only remaining way to mange healthcare costs is by asking people to take care of themselves. To do this, both patients and their caregivers must truly understand health information.

Individuals can make a difference. Health literacy can begin with just one person— a "health literacy advocate" perhaps—who needs no convincing why health literacy is important. This person can make a difference by learning about health literacy, raising awareness with colleagues and supervisors, and building a team to take action.

Teams can make a difference. Often, teams can more easily sustain health literacy efforts and make a lasting difference. As a team, individuals and organizations can come up with realistic ways of dealing with health communication problems. For example, a medical center might work with a local literacy program to test the readability of patient education materials.

At a minimum, health literacy teams should include subject-matter experts (like health providers, public health officials, administrators, and scientists), creators of health materials (such as writers, web developers, and media producers), and those who represent the intended audience (including community members, patients, and adult learners). Some of the most effective health literacy teams are partnerships of health facilities, community programs, and educational initiatives. Health literacy, indeed, goes beyond any one person, profession, or program.

People have difficulty understanding health information for a range of reasons including literacy, age, disability, language, culture, and emotion.

Sources to Learn More

Ad Hoc Committee on Health Literacy for the Council on Scientific Affairs, American Medical Association, 1999. Health literacy: Report of the Council on Scientific Affairs, *JAMA*, 281(6):552–557.

American Medical Association Foundation and the American Medical Association, 2003. *Health Literacy: Help your patients understand.* Available at http://www.ama-assn.org/ama/pub/category/9913.html. Accessed January 22, 2004.

Centre for Literacy of Quebec, 2001. *Health Literacy Project, Phase 1: Needs Assessment of the Health Education and Information Needs of Hard-to-Reach Patients.* Available at http://www.nald.ca/litcent.htm. Accessed January 23, 2004.

Davis TC, Williams MV, Marin E, Parker RM, Glass J, 2002. "Health literacy and cancer communication," *CA Cancer J Clin.*, 52:134–149.

Doak CC, Doak LG, Root JH, 1996. *Teaching Patients with Low Literacy Skills*, 2nd ed. Philadelphia, PA: J.B. Lippincott Company.

Center for Health Care Strategies, Inc., 2003. *Fact Sheets on Health Literacy.* Center for Health Care Strategies, Inc. Includes a series of nine fact sheets covering topics like "What is Health Literacy, "Who has health literacy problems," and the "Impact of low health literacy skills on annual health care expenditures." Available at http://www.chcs.org. Accessed January 23, 2004.

Healthy People 2010. Available at http://www.healthypeople.gov. Accessed January 31, 2004.

Institute of Medicine, 2004. *Health Literacy: A Prescription to End Confusion.* Washington, D.C.: The National Academies Press.

Kickbusch IS, 2001. "Health literacy: Addressing the health and education divide," *Health Promotion International*, 16(3):289–297.

Literacy in the information age: Final report of the international adult literacy survey, 2000. Statistics Canada. Available at http://www.statcan.ca/start.html. Accessed January 22, 2004.

McGee J, 1999. *Writing and Designing Print Materials for Beneficiaries: A Guide for State Medicaid Agencies.* HCFA Publication Number 10145. Baltimore, MD: Centers for Medicare & Medicaid Services, U.S. Department of Health and Human Services. (A second edition is forthcoming in 2004. For ordering information, contact Jeanne McGee, McGee & Evers Consulting, Inc., Vancouver, Washington, 360-574-4744, jmcgee@pacifier.com).

Nutbeam D, 1998. "Health promotion glossary," *Health Promotion International*, 13(4):349–364.

_____, 2000. "Health literacy as a public health goal: A challenge for contemporary health education and communication strategies into the 21st century." *Health Promotion International*, 15(3):259–267.

Osborne H, 2002. "In other words… health-literacy partnerships… working together can make a difference," *On Call* magazine, 5(9):16–17. Available at http://www.healthliteracy.com. Accessed January 23, 2004. Information is adapted and reprinted with permission of *On Call* magazine. *On Call* is published by Boston Works, a division of the *Boston Globe*.

_____, 2001. "In other words… know when to speak and when to listen… communicating with people who are anxious or angry," *On Call* magazine, 4(8):34–35. Available at http://www.healthliteracy.com. Accessed January 23, 2004. Information is adapted and reprinted with permission of *On Call* magazine. *On Call* is published by Boston Works, a division of the *Boston Globe*.

Parker RM, Ratzan SC, Lurie N, 2003. "Health literacy: A policy challenge for advancing high-quality health care," *Health Affairs*, 22(4):147–153.

Ratzan SC, 2001. "Health literacy: Communication for the public good," *Health Promotion International*, 16(2):207–214.

Singleton K, 2002. "Health literacy and adult English language learners," *ERIC Q&A*. Available at http://www.cal.org/ncle/digests/healthlitQA.htm. Accessed January 23, 2004.

Sullivan E, 2000. "Health literacy," *National Network of Libraries of Medicine*. Available at http://www.nnlm.gov/scr/conhlth/hlthlit.htm. Accessed January 23, 2004.

World Health Organization, Fifty-fourth World Health Assembly, 30 March 2001. Available at http://www.who.int/gb/EB_WHA/PDF/WHA54/ea548.pdf. Accessed January 23, 2004.

Assessing Literacy in Healthcare

Starting Points

Many adults cannot read or read well. They lack the literacy skills necessary to understand written healthcare materials like pamphlets, health histories, satisfaction surveys, informed consent documents, prescription labels, insurance bills, and even websites.

Defined in functional terms, literacy is the ability to use "printed and written information to function in society, to achieve one's goals, and to develop one's knowledge and potential" (Kirsch, et al., 1993). The most recent United States National Adult Literacy Survey, performed in 1992, found that nearly half of all adults in the United States have either inadequate or marginal literacy skills (Kirsch, et al., 1993). This indicates that people have trouble reading text and using documents that are complex or require specialized knowledge. The United States is not the only nation where functional literacy is problematic. The 1994 International Adult Literacy Survey (IALS) found comparable results when looking at literacy levels of adults in 20 countries around the world.

Literacy matters in healthcare because potentially harmful or life-threatening mistakes may happen when people cannot read or understand written healthcare information. Studies find that the readability of most healthcare materials is at a tenth grade level or above—a level that exceeds most people's ability to understand. "Jane," for example, reads at a fourth grade level. She is asked to fill out a health history form before seeing her new primary care provider. Since Jane has limited literacy skills, she simply checks "no" to all questions about illnesses and allergies. She knows from experience that this is one way to avoid a lot of follow-up questions. Jane's strategy, however, has costly consequences when her provider unknowingly prescribes a medication to which she is allergic.

To prevent errors like these, health providers agree that it is important to know about patients' literacy skills. However, providers and health literacy experts dispute the value of routine literacy testing in healthcare. On one side of the argument, some providers say that literacy tests help them know which teaching tools to use. If Jane's provider knew that she could barely read, perhaps the provider could give her a health history form that has a lot of pictures.

On the other side, many providers argue that formal literacy assessments do more harm than good. They feel that literacy tests needlessly raise patients' anxiety and expose feelings of shame. Also, many providers do not have easier-to-read versions of teaching materials and so cannot make use of literacy test results. These providers feel that noticing literacy "red flags" is sufficient to determine the best ways to communicate.

Archie Willard is an adult learner who learned to read when he was 54 years old. Here is what he says about formal literacy testing in healthcare settings:

There are those in the medical field who feel literacy testing should be done to receive medical attention. From your view point it looks like a good idea, but you need to look through the eyes of the person who has literacy problems. As a dyslexic and an adult learner with reading problems, I speak for many other adult learners. We hate having to take another written literacy test. People with other kinds of handicaps are not continually asked to expose their weaknesses to whatever degree they are handicapped. There is no physical pain in taking a written test, but when we have to there is a lot of frustration inside each of us. We grew up feeling humiliated because we had poor literacy skills and now we are adults. More written tests are seen as another step backward for us and it turns us away.

Strategies, Ideas, and Suggestions

Formal literacy assessments. Whether or not you favor formal literacy testing in health settings, you benefit in being familiar with the two of the most well-regarded assessment tools. They are:

- The REALM (Rapid Estimate of Adult Literacy in Medicine)—a reading recognition test that asks patients to pronounce 66 words ranging in difficulty from "fat" to "impetigo." This easy-to-administer test provides grade level scores for people who read below a ninth-grade level (Davis, et al., 1993).

- The TOFHLA (Test of Functional Health Literacy in Adults) and the S-TOFHLA (a shortened version) both include a series of health-related reading tasks that measure numeracy and reading comprehension. Like the REALM, this test is fairly easy to administer (Nurss, et al., 1995, Baker, 1995).

Informal literacy assessments. You can assess literacy informally by noticing "red flags" of literacy difficulties. These include when people:

- Always have "headaches" or chronically "forget" their eyeglasses when asked to perform reading tasks.
- Regularly bring family members or friends to help with paperwork.
- Identify their medications by looking at the pills rather than prescription labels.
- Ask a lot of questions about topics already covered in handouts and brochures.

Formal and informal literacy assessments together. Instead of always (or never) formally testing all patients, you might want to perform both formal and informal assessments. I remember working with a woman who was repeatedly hospitalized because she didn't adhere to her diabetes treatment plan. While I hadn't noticed any literacy red flags, her medical condition was so serious that the treatment team wanted to be sure this was not due to low literacy. When she read all 66 words on the REALM without problem, the treatment team looked for other explanations why this woman did not follow her treatment plan.

Ask patients how they like to learn. Beyond formally or informally assessing literacy, ask patients about their preferred learning styles. For example, you could ask "Do you like to learn by reading, watching TV, listening to the radio, or talking with family or friends?" If a patient chooses a non-reading option, you might follow up with a more specific question such as, "This new medicine has a lot of side effects to know about. To learn more, would you like a booklet or audiotape?"

Assessing Literacy in Healthcare

Have a variety of ways to communicate. Given literacy statistics, it is no surprise that many patients have trouble reading. To meet the needs of most people, strive to write health materials in plain language at a fifth to eighth grade reading level. Admittedly, this is not always possible when multi-syllabic words like "diabetes" and "chemotherapy" need to be included. If this is the case, beyond offering easy-to-read materials in plain language, provide non-written alternatives such as audiotapes, pictures, and objects or models. (To learn more, go to Plain Language on page 179.)

If it works, don't fix it. Even when you sense that a person cannot read or read well, you don't necessarily need to intervene. People with lifelong literacy problems most likely have developed coping strategies to manage reading tasks. "Sam," for example, always asks his wife to fill out his healthcare forms. You might need to take action only if his wife is not available to help. When a person's coping strategies work, perhaps you can safely put the literacy issues aside for now.

Literacy matters in healthcare because life–threatening or potentially harmful mistakes may happen when people cannot read or understand written information.

Sources to Learn More

Baker D, Williams M, Parker R, Gazmarian J, Nurss J,1999. "Development of a brief test to measure functional health literacy," *Patient Education and Counseling*, 38:33–42 (S-TOFHLA).

Davis T, Long S, Jackson R, Mayeaux E, et al., 1993. "Rapid estimate of adult literacy in medicine: A shortened screening instrument," *Clinical Research and Methods*, 25(6):391–395 (REALM).

Doak CC, Doak LG, Root JH, 1996. *Teaching Patients with Low Literacy Skills*, 2nd ed. Philadelphia, PA: J.B. Lippincott Company.

International Adult Literacy Survey (IALS). Available at http://www.nald.ca/nls/ials/introduc.htm. Accessed January 17, 2004.

Kirsch IS, Jungeblut A, Jenkins L, Kolstad A, 1993. Adult literacy in America: A first look at the results of the national adult literacy survey. National Center for Education Statistics. Washington, D.C.: U.S. Department of Education. Available at http://nces.ed.gov/naal. Accessed January 17, 2004.

NIFL-Health, an online discussion group about health literacy sponsored by the National Institute for Literacy. Available at http://www.nifl.gov/lincs. Accessed January 17, 2004.

Nurss JR, Parker RM, Williams MV, Baker DW, 1995. Test of functional health literacy in adults. Atlanta, GA: Emory University (TOFHLA).

Osborne H, 2004." In other words... adult learners and healthcare communication," *On Call* magazine, 7(3):16–17. Available at http://www.healthliteracy.com. Accessed May 3, 2004. Information is adapted and reprinted with permission of *On Call* magazine. *On Call* is published by BostonWorks, a division of the *Boston Globe*.

Assessing Readability

Starting Points

Many people say they write easy to read material. When asked how they know, most everyone says they use reading grade-level formulas (also called readability assessment tools). I often cringe when hearing this—especially if people rely solely on the formulas that are in their word processing programs. While arguably better than nothing, reading grade-level formulas are an imperfect and incomplete way to assess readability.

Over one hundred factors impact how readable any given document is, including the length of its sentences, choice of words, organization, tone, layout, use of illustrations, and meaning to the reader. Most reading formulas, however, only look at two or three of these factors. Commonly, the formulas calculate grade level based on the number of words in sentences and the number of syllables in words. While these formulas work well when used as originally intended—to help classroom teachers choose textbooks for students—they are not necessarily as effective when assessing health materials meant for adults.

One reason why reading grade-level formulas are less useful in health settings is that most adults read three to five grade levels below their last completed year of school. This means that someone with a high school education may better understand materials written at an eighth grade level. Another reason why formulas are inadequate is that sometimes people understand even "hard" words—especially when these words are clearly explained and of personal relevance. For example, a parent with limited literacy skills whose child has asthma may understand the word "bronchodilator" despite its many syllables.

Despite their drawbacks, reading grade-level formulas are objective, easy-to-use, and the scores almost always get people's attention. In fact, I often use them at the beginning of projects to compare a document's readability with local or national literacy statistics. When the gap between these figures is too wide to ignore, projects often get the funding and administrative "go ahead" they need. (You can find adult literacy estimates by state, county, congressional district, and city or town online at www.casas.org/lit/litcode/Search.cfm).

In addition to reading grade-level formulas, checklists provide another way to assess readability. Often, the checklists have criteria specific to a facility or an audience. Checklist questions might include:

- When, along the continuum of care, will this material be distributed?
- Does the material consider the culture of our patient population?
- How else can our patients learn this information?

Feedback from readers is by far the most effective assessment tool for readability. Truly, they are the experts on what is understandable.

> Just because a document is statistically readable doesn't mean that people can really understand. Readability formulas don't tell you everything. People often have trouble with complicated ideas or documents that overload readers with too much information.
>
> —Mark Hochhauser PhD, readability consultant.

Strategies, Ideas, and Suggestions

Readability goals and how to meet them. To be understood by "average" readers, most health literacy experts recommend that materials be written at a fifth to eighth grade reading level. As a writer, however, I know that this goal is sometimes hard to meet. My rule of thumb in writing is to lower the reading level as much as possible while also keeping true to the content. Generally, this means using one- and two-syllable words whenever possible. When longer technical words are truly needed, I define them in plain language. For example, "Clinical trials (research studies with people who have cancer)."

For material to be truly easy-to-read, its reading level must match the reader's literacy skills. I almost always feel confident that I have met this readability goal when readers confirm that they understand and can make use of the written information.

Assessing readability "by hand." The SMOG (Statistical Measurement of Gobbledygook) and the Fry Readability Formula are two well-regarded reading grade-level tools that can be done by hand (with pencil and paper). While both formulas give grade-level scores, they calculate them in different ways. The SMOG counts all words with three or more syllables in three ten-sentence passages. The Fry formula looks at the number of syllables and sentences in three 100-word passages. You can find online instructions for both of these tools at the websites listed in Sources to Learn More.

Assessing readability by hand only takes a few minutes and has several advantages over computer-based formulas. One is that you can assess any document, whether it is in your computer or not. Another is that you can add a dose of common sense, such as deciding whether a particular group of words is really a sentence. Also, you can quickly see problem areas. With the SMOG, for example, multi-syllabic words are obvious since you circle all words with three or more syllables.

An area of dispute about readability formulas is whether it is okay to amend the rules and count repetitive, yet necessary, multi-syllabic words (like "diabetes") only once instead of each time they appear in the text. While I appreciate that fiddling with the formula like this may lower the reading grade level, in my opinion this method causes as many problems as it solves. For example, once you change this rule you then must create a new one about which multi-syllabic words to count. Instead, my method is to follow all the formula's rules but mention in the summary report why the grade-level score is as high as it is.

Checklists. Checklists, created by you or developed by others, can be very useful to assess how well written material matches the specific needs of its intended readers. Used throughout the writing process, checklists can identify a material's strengths, weaknesses, and areas to revise. Checklist criteria can include factors such as content, design, source credibility, organization, language, tone, appearance, graphics, and cultural considerations.

You can almost always adapt checklists to fit your needs. While you may sometimes use an entire checklist, at other times you might use just part of it or assess just one aspect of a document. Two well-regarded checklists are the SAM (Suitability of Assessment of Materials) (Doak, Doak, and Root, 1996) and the Guide Checklist for Assessing Print Materials (McGee, 1999). (To learn more, go to Feedback: Interviews and Focus Groups on page 57.)

Assessing readability by computer. Many word processing programs include readability statistics in the spelling and grammar check. Admittedly, assessing readability this way is fast and easy. There are limitations, however, in that these computer-based assessment tools are only as smart as the people who program them. You can get more meaningful results with computer-based assessments when you first prepare the text. Here's how:

- Choose materials that are sufficiently long, with at least 30 sentences or 300 words. Then assess at least three passages that represent the entire document—one each from the beginning, middle, and end. Avoid the first and last sentences, however, as these passages tend to be easier to read than other text.

- Remove headings, titles, subtitles, and bullet points. This way, the computer doesn't give artificially low scores by counting sentence fragments as complete sentences. In this book, for example, the heading "Strategies, Ideas, and Suggestions" might be mistakenly counted as a sentence.

- Take out all mid-sentence punctuation such as periods, colons, and semi-colons. You need to do this because most computer-based assessments recognize sentences as groups of words that end with punctuation. While you know that "John has a temperature of 98.2." is one sentence, the computer may count it as two.

You might also want to buy software designed specifically to assess readability. Ones that are often recommended include:

- Readability Calculations, www.micropowerandlight.com
- Grammar Expert Plus, www.wintertree-software.com
- Spell Catcher Plus, www.spellcatcher.com

Making sense of readability assessment scores. Whatever reading grade-level formula or tool you use, be cautious not to over-interpret the results. At best, grade-level scores are only accurate by plus or minus one and a half grade levels. This means that when a score drops from 7.3 to 6.8, the document is not necessarily easier to read. Results may also vary depending on which formula you use. For example, the Fry formula often scores materials one to two grade levels lower than the SMOG.

Don't write "to the formula." Reading grade-level formulas are better used to predict reading difficulty than as guides for good writing. In fact, a document with a "good" readability score isn't always easy to read. Its text may be so choppy that it is unappealing and hard to understand. To make written materials truly readable use plain language principles, have information that readers need to know and organize it from the reader's point of view. (To learn more, go to Plain Language on page 179.)

Test materials with intended readers. Readability assessment tools alone are not sufficient. The best way to know whether documents are truly easy to read is by asking intended readers. You might find interested and appropriate volunteers by teaming up with your community's literacy council or with your workplace's employee education program. From the first idea to the final draft, ask people what they want and need to know and then test your document to make sure readers can truly understand. (To learn more, go to Feedback: Interviews and Focus Groups on page 57.)

Materials in other languages. Many people ask about assessing readability in other languages. In truth, this is a challenge because each language has its own word and sentence structure. Start with an easy-to-read English version and then give translators flexibility in language and design so as to maintain readability. Have the material translated back into English to confirm that the key points are intact. And then, as with all materials, test it with intended readers. (To learn more, go to Translations on page 231.)

While arguably better than nothing, reading grade-level formulas are an imperfect and incomplete way to assess readability.

Sources to Learn More

Chall JS, Dale E, 1995. *Readability Revisited: The New Dale-Chall Readability Formula.* Cambridge, MA: Brookline Books.

Doak CC, Doak LG, Root JH, 1996. *Teaching Patients with Low Literacy Skills,* 2nd ed. Philadelphia, PA: J.B. Lippincott Company.

The Fry Readability Formula is available at the Center for Disease Control, Human Subjects Research website at http://www.cdc.gov/od/ads/fry.htm. Accessed January 17, 2004.

Gilliam B, Pena SC, Mountain L, 1980. "The Fry graph applied to Spanish readability," *The Reading Teacher,* January:426–431.

Hochhauser M, 2003. "How to make forms and notices understandable—and compliant," *Patient Care Management,* 19(8):7–8.

McGee J, 1999. *Writing and Designing Print Materials for Beneficiaries: A Guide for State Medicaid Agencies.* HCFA Publication Number 10145. Baltimore, MD: Centers for Medicare & Medicaid Services, U.S. Department of Health and Human Services. (A second edition is forthcoming in 2004. For ordering information, contact Jeanne McGee, McGee & Evers Consulting, Inc., Vancouver, Washington, 360-574-4744, jmcgee@pacifier.com).

Osborne H, 2000. "In other words. . .assessing readability. . .rules for playing the numbers game," *On Call* magazine, 3(12):38–39. Available at http://www.healthliteracy.com. Information is adapted and reprinted with permission of *On Call* magazine. *On Call* is published by BostonWorks, a division of the *Boston Globe.*

Micro Power and Light, 1995. *Readability Calculations* software. Includes the Dale-Chall, Reading Ease, Flesch Grade Level, FOG, and the Powers-Sumner-Kearl formulas. Available at http://www.micropowerandlight.com. Accessed January 17, 2004.

Rugimbana R, Patel C, 1996. "The application of the marketing concept in textbook selection: Using the Cloze procedure," *Journal of Marketing Education,* Spring:14–20.

Rosenblum LR, 1995. *Assessing Breast and Cervical Cancer Education Materials for Literacy Level and Cultural Appropriateness.* Boston, MA: World Education, Inc.

The SMOG formula is available at the Center for Disease Control, Human Subjects Research website at http://www.cdc.gov/od/ads/smog.htm. Accessed January 17, 2004.

Assessing Readability

Bulleted Lists

Starting Points

Bulleted lists combine visual cues and text to focus attention, organize data, and present information in "bite-sized nuggets." These lists include several elements: text lead-ins that introduce bulleted lists, bullet points that visually mark all items, and listed items which are sometimes accompanied by explanatory text.

Bulleted lists are used in many industries and settings:

We used bulleted lists with check-off boxes as 'job aids' in our factory. They gave workers a visual picture of the action-oriented steps they needed to complete. When they checked off the boxes, workers had a sense of completion and could easily see that their job was done.

—Mary Schutten, former training manager at
Boeing Commercial Airplane Company

Bulleted lists can be equally effective in healthcare, as readers can quickly see the information they need to know and do. For example, lists can be about how to prevent injury, self-care tasks, symptoms and side effects, or when to call a health professional.

Strategies, Ideas, and Suggestions

Bullets. Bullets visually mark all listed items. Often, they are darkened circles like the ones that appear throughout this book. Other options are arrows, squares, numbers, or fancy designs (also called "dingbats"). Choose bullets to suit your purpose. For example, you might use numbers when writing about sequential steps, or check-off boxes when you want readers to mark when they take certain actions. Here are some commonly-used bullets found in Microsoft Word™:

- Darkened circle
- ❏ Check-off box
- → Arrow
- ∴ Design

Text lead-ins. Begin each bulleted list with a brief text lead-in that introduces readers to the information that follows. Lead-ins can be short phrases or complete sentences. They can also be used to avoid redundancy when all listed items begin the same way.

For example, instead of:

Here are some ways to eat well:
- You can drink a glass of water when you wake up
- You can eat fish at least twice a week

- You can have raw vegetables for snacks between meals
- You can buy whole-grain rather than white bread

You can reduce redundancy with this text lead-in:

Here are some ways to eat well. You can:
- Drink a glass of water when you wake up
- Eat fish at least twice a week
- Have raw vegetables for snacks between meals
- Buy whole-grain rather than white bread

Consistency. All bulleted items should be parallel, meaning that they must be structured in similar ways. Each bullet should begin with the same part of speech. Commonly, this is an action verb like "do" or "know," or a gerund (word ending in "ing") such as "learning" or "understanding."

Likewise, grammar and punctuation should be consistent. Decide whether all items start with capital or lowercase letters, and whether items should end with a period or no punctuation at all.

Explanatory text. My preferred style, similar to that used in this book, is to start items with a few-word phrase, followed by an explanation that make take several sentences. To me, this combination helps people scan for what they need and offers additional information for those who want to learn more.

Length of lists. Generally, lists should have between three and eight items. A single item shouldn't be bulleted and two items can often be written as a sentence rather than a list. If your list is too long, sort or "chunk" information into sub-categories—each with their own headings.

For example, instead of one long list:

Fruit:

- Banana
- Cantaloupe
- Casaba
- Grapefruit
- Honeydew
- Lemons
- Limes
- Mango
- Oranges
- Papaya
- Pineapple
- Pomegranate
- Tangerines
- Watermelon

You can have three shorter lists:

Citrus Fruit

- Grapefruit
- Lemons
- Limes
- Oranges
- Tangerines

Melons

- Cantaloupe
- Casaba
- Honeydew
- Watermelon

Tropical Fruit

- Banana
- Mango
- Papaya
- Pineapple
- Pomegranate

Layout. Generally, it is easier to read bulleted lists when there is a blank line between sections. Justify (line up) lists on the left rather than centering them on a page so the reader always looks in the same starting place. Try, also, not to have a list within a list. If you truly need to do so, use different bullets as well as indentation to differentiate between the two.

Color. If your budget allows, you might want to add color to bullet points. For example, you could use colored traffic-light bullets in green, yellow, and red to indicate go, caution, and stop. Make sure, however, that these bullet points make sense even without color so people who are color-blind or see reprints only in black and white can understand them.

Bulleted lists combine visual cues and text to focus attention, organize data, and present information in "bite-sized nuggets" that readers can understand.

Sources to Learn More

Doak CC, Doak LG, Root JH, 1996. *Teaching Patients with Low Literacy Skills,* 2nd ed. Philadelphia, PA: J.B. Lippincott Company.

McGee J, 1999. *Writing and Designing Print Materials for Beneficiaries: A Guide for State Medicaid Agencies.* HCFA Publication Number 10145. Baltimore, MD: Centers for Medicare & Medicaid Services, U.S. Department of Health and Human Services. (A second edition is forthcoming in 2004. For ordering information, contact Jeanne McGee, McGee & Evers Consulting, Inc., Vancouver, Washington, 360-574-4744, jmcgee@pacifier.com).

Plain Language Action & Information Network (a government-wide group) includes the resource "Writing user-friendly documents" available at http://www.plainlanguage.gov. Accessed January 18, 2004.

Say What You Mean on the Web includes the report, "12 tips for bulleted lists," available at http://www.ronscheer.com/index.html. Accessed January 18, 2004.

Choosing, Adapting, and Reviewing Teaching Materials

Starting Points

Rather than always writing your own teaching materials, you may find it more economic and efficient to use "as is" ones that others have created. This way, you can save the time and money of starting from scratch (though you may have associated costs for copies or reprint and licensing fees). Be sure, however, to allow sufficient time to obtain any needed copyright or reprint permissions.

Sometimes you may want to modify or adapt already-existing materials to better suit your needs. For example, you may want to insert the names of several local homecare services in your list of resources, or add drawings and examples from your patient population's culture.

Regardless if you use material as is or adapt it, review the material on a regular basis to ensure that information is accurate, up-to-date, and matches your patient's learning, literacy, and language needs.

> When the Thoracic Unit at the Massachusetts General Hospital in Boston, MA wanted patient education materials for tracheotomy teaching, the staff decided to blend a commercially-available illustration with an instruction sheet written "in house." This way, patients benefit by getting a full-color, anatomic illustration along with a handout explaining specifically what they need to know and do.
>
> —Taryn Pittman, RN, MSN, Patient Education Specialist
> at the Massachusetts General Hospital in Boston, MA

Strategies, Ideas, and Suggestions

Low-cost and free materials. Government agencies, national associations, and even pharmaceutical companies can be good sources for free or low-cost materials. Review the information from these groups carefully, however, to make sure that the ones you want are unbiased and contain no advertising. If the material you choose promotes a particular product or point of view, alert readers to this fact first, and consider supplementing it with unbiased information from other sources such as government agencies or national associations.

Commercial publishers. Commercial publishers produce many excellent materials but these are sometimes quite costly. Before making a purchase, you may want to talk with the company's sales representative. Ask if there are discounts for large orders or as incentives for future business.

Web-based information. The Internet offers a wealth of information, though the quality is not assured. One way to find reliable content is to begin with web addresses that end in ".edu," ".gov," or ".org" (rather than ".com"). While the first three endings do not guarantee quality, the information tends not to be swayed by commercial interests. Check credentials by reading about the sponsoring organization as well as information on the writer(s), contributor(s), and members of the editorial board on the site's "About Us" page.

Adapting from others. Sometimes, there is material that you feel would be even better with just a few changes. You might, for example, want to use rural rather than urban examples or make audiotape recordings of written materials for patients with limited literacy or vision.

Before you use materials (even website information) as is or adapt them, contact the author or publisher and ask permission to do so. You may be asked to pay a reprint or licensing fee and include a specific tagline. For instance, a publisher might want you to cite attribution by adding, "Reprinted and adapted with permission from XYZ Publishers." Allow sufficient lead-time as permission to reprint and adapt can take weeks or even months.

Choosing materials. Invite clinicians, members of your patient education committee, and other subject-matter experts to help review and select teaching materials. Ask patients for their feedback, as well. After all, patients are the best ones to judge whether materials are understandable, meaningful, useful, appealing, and relevant. To help people participate in this review process, you might want to provide a checklist of important items to consider. Items can include:

- **Authorship.** Is the material from a dependable source? Do the authors have subject-matter expertise? Are the references credible?

- **Content.** Is the information accurate, comprehensive, patient-oriented, and relevant? Does the material have mostly need-to-know content about skills and behaviors rather than nice-to-know background information? Is there a list of print, phone, online, and in-person resources for people to learn more?

- **Currency.** Is the material accurate and up-to-date? For books, videos and CDs, this generally means that they were produced within the last 5 years. For websites, it often is whether the information was posted or updated in the past year.

- **Language.** Is the material written in a tone and at a reading level that readers can relate to and understand? Is the material in plain language, using common words that readers already know and defining ones they need to learn? (To learn more, go to Plain Language on page 179.)

- **Visuals.** Does the material look appealing? Are the drawings and illustrations age-appropriate? Is the material easy to see? Generally, this means that: there is sufficient white space (about a 50/50 mix of print and blank space), the type size is at least 12-point and even larger for readers who are older or have limited vision, there are headings that clearly identify all sections, and, visuals enhance—not distract from—the text. (To learn more, go to Visuals on page 245.)

- **Culture.** Do the words and examples match the logic, language, and experience of your readers? Are the images and examples realistic and do they present the culture in a positive way? Is the material available in the needed languages? (To learn more, go to Language and Culture: Communicating with People from Other Languages and Lands on page 123.)

- **Interactive Features.** Are interactive features (like check-off boxes, fill-in-the blank exercises, quizzes, or log sheets) easy to use? For example, a medication log sheet should be designed large enough so that people with limited dexterity can easily write in the allotted spaces.

- **Personal relevance.** Does the material motivate readers and encourage them to take action? Does the content match the readers' needs and goals? For example, when choosing a brochure about fitness for older adults, consider whether your readers are more motivated by being independent or by living longer. If they're more interested in independence, you might choose a brochure that links exercise with walking to the grocery store rather than one that highlights ways to live fifteen more years.

Invite clinicians, members of your patient education committee, and other subject-matter experts to help review and select teaching materials. Ask patients for their feedback, as well. After all, patients are the best ones to judge whether materials are understandable, meaningful, useful, appealing, and relevant.

Sources to Learn More

AMC Cancer Research Center, 1994. *Beyond the Brochure: Alternative Approaches to Effective Health Communication.* Center for Disease Control and Prevention. Available at http://www.cdc.gov/cancer/nbccedp. Accessed January 24, 2004.

Osborne H, 2002. "In other words... making it work... selecting healthcare brochures for older adults," *On Call* magazine, 5(10):16–17. Available at http://www.healthliteracy.com. Accessed January 18, 2004. Information is adapted and reprinted with permission of *On Call* magazine. *On Call* is published by BostonWorks, a division of the *Boston Globe*.

———, 2002. "In other words…making the match…choosing patient education materials," *On Call* magazine, 5(1):30–31. Available at http://www.healthliteracy.com. Accessed January 18, 2004. Information is adapted and reprinted with permission of *On Call* magazine. *On Call* is published by BostonWorks, a division of the *Boston Globe*.

Consumer Health Libraries

Starting Points

Consumer health libraries, sometimes called learning or resource centers, have collections of credible, up-to-date health materials for the general public, patients, and their families. They may also be used by health professionals and educators who want teaching materials to use with their patients and students. Whether you work in a medical center, public library, or community agency, you might consider starting or maintaining a consumer health library that helps consumers better understand information specific to their health needs.

In today's society, people have to be their own health advocates. There's so much information out there with a lot of conflicting studies. It can get confusing and people need credible, good information.

—Ayako Barnum, a librarian who oversees HELP (Health Education Library Project) at the Morse Institute Library in Natick, MA

Strategies, Ideas, and Suggestions

Location, location, location. Make sure your consumer health library is in a convenient location that is not only safe but also easy to get to by walking, driving, or public transportation. If your library is housed within a larger facility like a medical center, try to find a space that is in a high traffic area. This way, even patients and visitors who hadn't planned to go to the library may be tempted to visit. And if your library is not centrally located, have signs and maps letting people know where to go and how to get there.

Some medical facilities have several consumer health libraries instead of just one. For example, they may have a collection of women's health materials in the internal medicine waiting room and cancer-related materials near where people check in for their chemotherapy appointments.

Library users. Consumer health libraries appeal to people of all ages, interests, learning abilities, and levels of health knowledge. The general public, for example, may be interested in basic nutrition and exercise information. Patients and families may instead want to know more about a particular diagnosis, medication, or treatment. Your library may also appeal to teachers, clinicians, and community health educators who want off-the-shelf teaching materials they can use in health education classes.

Services. Some consumer health libraries, such as ones based in public libraries, offer only information. Others, especially those in hospitals and health centers, might also have patient educators available to teach skills and lead classes. Regardless of its scope, let library users know about all your library services. But also make it clear that the library is for general information only and that people should talk with their health providers about specific medical conditions and treatment options.

Staff and behind-the-scenes support. Staff may include professional librarians, health providers, and trained volunteers who help consumers find needed information at levels and in formats they can use and understand. Behind the scenes a team of administrators, clinicians, educators, librarians, volunteers, marketing folks, business leaders, technical advisors, patients, families, and the general public often collaborate to create and maintain a consumer health library that truly meets the learning and teaching needs of its community.

Welcome visitors. Newcomers to your library may feel awkward when they first visit. Perhaps they don't know where to begin their information search or maybe they are overwhelmed with too many choices. You can help by having a staff member (either a professional librarian or trained volunteer) greet people as they enter. This staff person not only can welcome visitors but also answer questions, help find information and, as needed, refer people to outside agencies and services.

Since it is unrealistic to assume that staff is always available to greet visitors, consider having a "Welcome Packet" for people as they enter. At the very least, this packet should include information about the library and who to contact with questions.

Build your collection. People learn in many ways. Some prefer reading; others learn by listening, hearing, seeing, or doing. Try to collect a variety of materials that meet these diverse needs. For example, you can have print materials in a range of reading levels (from easy-to-read to scientific), audio and video tapes, DVDs, CDs, models, folding displays, flip charts, and even puppets. Make sure to also have culturally appropriate materials that are translated into the languages most common in your local area.

Review materials. Library users often comment how much they value up-to-date health information. To keep your collection current, regularly review your materials to confirm that the information is accurate and reflects the latest in medical practice. Generally, this means reviewing your collection at least once every one to two years. When there are new scientific findings, you may want to review your collection even more often.

Information and referral resources. Realistically, consumer health libraries cannot be everything to everyone. One way to meet the needs of library users is to create a referral resource or directory. This can include the names and contact information of local social service agencies, support groups, and community-based advocacy programs. Make sure to update this resource list at least once a year, however, as organizations move and people change jobs.

Teaching about the Internet. Beyond the materials in your library's collection, you might also want to teach library users how to access and evaluate Internet (website) health information. One way you can do this is by writing a consumer guide. Topics might include: how to search online for information, ways to evaluate websites, and things to remember when reading health-related web pages.

Community outreach. Marketing and public relations are important aspects of consumer health libraries. You can help "spread the word" about your library by writing press releases and having displays at local community events. You might also want to write a newsletter or "e-zine" (electronic magazine) that is distributed to local residents or subscribers who want to know more. Your library's website (or web page) can also be linked to other agencies and community organizations. Ask local organizations to post bulletin board notices about your library and offer to reciprocate with information about their services. Word-of-mouth referrals are especially important. It's very powerful when one neighbor says to another, "You really should visit the consumer health library—they have a lot of useful information."

Evaluation and feedback. Consumer health libraries work best when they partner with the people they serve. Ask those who use your library (and those who don't, but could) about the materials and services they want and need. You can gather this feedback formally through written surveys or informally by talking with users about their wants, needs, and interests.

Networking. Join or start a consumer health network of local organizations that agree to share resources and promote each other's services. For example, this network could include a public library, hospital, nursing school, literacy program, and senior center. Consider, too, being part of a network of consumer health librarians. This network can be a forum to share concerns, to learn from each other, and to brainstorm ways to manage volunteers, collect materials, and reach out to the community.

Be sure to have culturally appropriate materials that are translated into the languages most common in your local area.

Sources to Learn More

CAPHIS (Consumer and Patient Health Information) has a wealth of information for consumers and librarians alike. This includes a "Top 100 List" of recommended consumer health websites. The site also has many articles, links, and resources about managing consumer health libraries. Available at http://www.caphis.mlanet.org. Accessed January 18, 2004.

Longe ME, Thomas K, 1998. *Consumer Health Resource Centers: A Guide to Successful Planning and Implementation.* Chicago, IL: American Hospital Publishing, Inc.

MEDLINEplus Health Information, a service of the U.S. National Library of Medicine and the National Institutes of Health, includes drug dictionaries and encyclopedias, updates on research results on a broad range of diseases, tutorials and a clinical trials database. For many librarians, this site is a "first stop" for consumer health information. Available at http://medlineplus.gov. Accessed January 18, 2004.

Pittman TJ, O'Connor MD, Millar S, Erikson JI, 2001. "Patient education: Designing a state-of-the-art consumer health information library," *Journal of Nursing Administration,* 31(6):316–323.

Rees AM, 2000. *Consumer Health Information Source Book.* Phoenix, AZ: Oryx Press.

Schloman BF, 2002. "Quality of health information on the web: Where are we now?," *Online Journal of Issues in Nursing,* December 16.

Decision Aids and Shared Decision-Making

Starting Points

Patients generally make their own treatment and healthcare decisions in the United States today. They usually do so after talking with their physicians and other health providers, learning about their options, and reflecting (perhaps with family, friends, and others in similar situations) about personal values and priorities.

In this process, often called "shared decision-making," providers present options, outcomes, probabilities, and uncertainties.

Patients, in turn, share their values and concerns as they relate to benefits and harms of treatment alternatives. Together, providers and patients plan a course of action.

Health decisions like these are usually difficult for patients to make. Decisions almost always have immediate and long-term implications, many of which are unknown or uncertain. Often patients must make these important decisions at times when they are stressed, scared, or in pain.

Decision aids can help. These tools are not only designed to present unbiased and evidence-based information about treatment choices but also help patients clarify their concerns about uncertainty and risk. Whether as books, videos, audio-guided workbooks, CD-ROMs, DVDs, or web-based applications, decision aids are intended to supplement, not replace or diminish, patient-provider conversations.

The CREDIBLE model, developed by Dr. Annette O'Connor at the Ottawa Health Research Institute in Canada, highlights objective criteria to consider when developing or choosing decision aids.

C - Is the decision aid competently developed?
R - Is the information recent (or recently updated)?
E - Is the information evidence-based?
DI - Is the decision aid devoid of conflicts of interest?
BL - Does it give a balanced presentation of options, benefits, and harms?
E - Is the decision aid efficacious and helpful?

Figure 1.1   The CREDIBLE Model   *Source: Reprinted with permission from Dr. O'Connor, Ottawa Health Research Institute*

Here's an example about how a decision-aid video can be used:

A woman diagnosed with early stage breast cancer often can choose whether to have breast-conserving surgery (such as a lumpectomy) followed by radiation, or a mastectomy. Besides discussing these options with her doctor, talking with family and friends, and reading about the topic, the woman can also watch a decision-aid video. This video not only has factual information about options, outcomes, and complications but also contains first-hand accounts from women who talk about the choices they made. Throughout the video there are opportunities to reflect on priorities and values. After watching, the woman is better-informed about her options and ready to make a treatment choice she feels is right for her.

Strategies, Ideas, and Suggestions

Shared decision-making. Decision-making conversations often start with an acknowledgment of the patient/provider partnership and the roles that each has in making decisions. The provider's role includes explaining alternatives and helping patients weigh the impact of each one. The patient's role is to learn about choices, consider personal values, and participate as actively in the decision-making process as he or she wants and is able.

Research data. Let patients know about potential risks and benefits of their choices. When you present data from clinical trials and research studies, make sure to discuss how to interpret these results. This means noting whether the studies are with people similar to them in terms of age, gender, race, and diagnosis. It also means making sense of ambiguous findings and unanswered questions.

Values. Help patients clarify their feelings and values, such as their tolerance for uncertainty. Talk about the personal impact of their choice including side effects, possibility for error, and long-term outcomes such as pain or disability. As well, find out how much patients want to be involved in decision-making. While many want to take an active role, others may look to their doctors, family members, or other trusted advisors for help in making decisions.

Risk perception. The decisions that people make depend, in large part, on how they perceive risk. Often, this is as much about feelings as it is facts. For example, someone desperate for hope may underestimate the likelihood that something will go wrong and overestimate the chance for a cure. Another person, familiar with a neighbor's experience in a similar situation, may be sure that his or her treatment outcome will be exactly the same. (To learn more, go to Risk Communication on page 193.)

Decision-making conversations often start with an acknowledgment of the patient/provider partnership and the roles that each has in making decisions.

Sources to Learn More

Bennett P, 1999. Communicating about risks to public health. *Centre for Environmental Research and Training*, England: University of Birmingham. Available at http://www.doh.gov.uk/pointers.htm. Accessed January 18, 2004.

Best Treatments. "Includes information for patients and doctors about evidence-based medicine, shared decision-making, and risk," *BMJ*. Available at http://www.besttreatments.org. Accessed January 18, 2004.

O'Connor AM, Legare F, Stacey D, 2003. "Risk communication in practice: The contribution of decision aids," *BMJ*, 327:736–740.

O'Connor A, Tait V, Stacey D, et al., 2003. "Communicating the benefits/harms of estrogen-progestin hormone therapy decision aids," *Medscape Women's Health eJournal*, 8(2), 2003. Available at http://www.medscape.com/viewarticle/450848. Accessed January 18, 2004.

O'Connor AM, et al., 1998. "A decision aid for women considering hormone therapy after menopause: Decision support framework and evaluation," *Patient Education and Counseling*, 33:267–279.

Osborne H, 2004. "In other words…helping patients make difficult decisions," *On Call* magazine, 7(4):16–17. Available at http://www.healthliteracy.com. Accessed May 15, 2004. Information is adapted and reprinted with permission of *On Call* magazine. *On Call* is published by BostonWorks, a division of the *Boston Globe*.

_____, 2002. *Partnering with Patients to Improve Health Outcomes*. Gaithersburg, MD: Aspen Publishers, Inc.

Ottawa Health Research Institute, includes "Guidelines for Developing Quality Patient Decision Aids According to the Pre-Set Criteria in the Cochrane Review." Available at www.ohri.ca. Accessed January 18, 2004.

Say RE, Thomson R, 2003. "The importance of patient preferences in treatment decisions—Challenges for doctors," *BMJ*, 327:542–545.

Email

Starting Points

Email is a comfortable and familiar communication tool for many people. A recent study found that more than 70% of Americans use the Internet and, of this group, 90% use email and instant messaging (UCLA, 2003).

Despite its widespread acceptance, email is not yet a tool widely used for patients and providers to communicate with each other. This will likely change soon, however, as people recognize the value of using email to efficiently and effectively communicate non-urgent medical information such as renewing prescriptions, scheduling appointments, and exchanging information about chronic medical conditions.

Email in healthcare provides many benefits. People may respond at their convenience, messages can be printed and saved, and hyperlinks can be added so people only need to click for more information. But email also brings concerns about privacy and security. For instance, people who share computers can sometimes access messages intended for others and employers can legally read messages their employees send from work.

Many patients and providers feel that the benefits of email outweigh its drawbacks. Used well and used wisely, email can be a powerful and effective health communication tool.

When email is used well, it can save patients and providers the time and expense of needless office visits. Here is an example:

In addition to treating patients in his Boston office, Dr. Sands also communicates with them by email. "Ann," for instance, is a sixty-year-old woman who lives about three hours away. While mowing her lawn, she was bitten on her finger by a wasp. Ann knew it wasn't an emergency but was concerned that her finger was infected when it swelled up and turned a fierce-looking red. She emailed Dr. Sands and attached digital photos of her finger.

Seeing this picture, Dr. Sands felt that Ann's reaction was only inflammatory and didn't require emergency treatment. He recommended she apply ice, elevate her hand, and email him again in 48 hours. He also wrote in his email reply that Ann should go to a local emergency department if her symptoms worsened. Two days later, Ann emailed back, "You were right. The bite already subsided."

From Daniel Z. Sands, MD, MPH, clinical director of electronic patient records and communication at Beth Israel Deaconess Medical Center in Boston, MA.

Strategies, Ideas, and Suggestions

Make it clear that email is not to be used for emergencies. Patients need to fully understand that email is not to be used for medical emergencies. There is no guarantee that providers will see messages quickly enough nor is there any assurance that patients will read responses in time to take immediate action.

Use plain language. Make sure your email messages are easy to read. This means using plain language principles such as common one- and two-syllable words, short sentences with no more than fifteen words, and short paragraphs with only two or three sentences. These principles are even more important when replying to patient's messages that have a lot of spelling, punctuation, and vocabulary errors—indications the writer may have problems with literacy or language. (To learn more, go to Plain Language on page 179.)

Replying to messages. Let patients know when to expect replies from you—such as within 24 hours, or one to two days. In addition, create an "auto responder" that automatically notifies patients when you receive their message. In this automated reply, include a phone number where patients can call for more immediate assistance.

Consider the most appropriate way to respond. Just because patients send you email messages doesn't mean you need to reply the same way. For example, email should not be used to convey bad news or discuss treatment options. Instead, you can use email to arrange phone or in-person appointments to talk about these more complex and sensitive issues.

Have a written agreement. Patients and providers alike should sign written agreements about using email. While these agreements may vary, at a minimum they should acknowledge that:

- you discussed benefits and drawbacks of email communication.
- patients received written guidelines, policies, and procedures.
- email from patients will be put in their medical records.
- email is not be used in medical emergencies.

For examples of written agreements, go to HealthyEmail at http://www.healthyemail.org.

Keep a record of email correspondence. Whether or not you put all of a patient's email messages into his or her medical record, make sure to keep some sort of log or file of each exchange. This provides a written record of your advice and the patient's response that may be needed should questions or legal disputes arise.

Privacy concerns. Alert patients as to how email is handled in your office, including who is authorized to read and triage messages. Be very cautious about sending group messages to all your patients, making sure to address each person as BCC (blind carbon-copy). If you email from a computer network or on a shared computer at home, create separate files or accounts so others cannot access the messages between you and patients.

Reimbursement. As yet, few insurance companies reimburse providers for time spent exchanging email with patients. But this situation may soon change as associations like the American Medical Association and the American College of Physicians are advocating that providers be reimbursed for this important and cost-saving service.

Patients and providers alike should sign written agreements about using email.

Sources to Learn More

Electronic Patient Centered Communication Resource Center Available at http://www.e-pcc.org. Accessed January 18, 2004.

Fox S, Fallows D, 2003. *Internet Health Resources, Pew Internet & American Life Project.* Available at http://www.pewinternet.org. Accessed January 28, 2004.

Guidelines for physician-patient electronic communications, 2003. American Medical Association. Available at http://www.ama-assn.org/ama/pub/category/2386.html. Accessed January 18, 2004.

HealthyEmail. Available at http://www.healthyemail.org. Accessed January 18, 2004.

Osborne H, 2003. "In other words...communicating electronically with patients," *On Call* magazine, 6(8):16–17. Available at http://www.healthliteracy.com. Accessed January 18, 2004. Information is adapted and reprinted with permission of *On Call* magazine. *On Call* is published by BostonWorks, a division of the *Boston Globe*.

Tate DF, Jackvony EH, Wing RR, 2003. "Effects of Internet behavioral counseling on weight loss in adults at risk for type 2 diabetes," *JAMA*, 289(14):1833–1836.

UCLA Internet report: Surveying the digital future, year three, 2003. Los Angeles: University of California. Available at http://ccp.ucla.edu/pdf/UCLA-Internet-Report-Year-Three.pdf. Accessed January 18, 2004.

Email

Ethics of Simplicity

Starting Points

In many ways, health professionals are translators of scientific and medical information—writing complicated, rapidly-changing, numbers-based information in a manner that is clear and simple enough for "average" readers to understand. This task is much more difficult than simply finding the right words to use. Indeed, there are many dilemmas to resolve and issues to consider when simplifying complex information. For example:

- Am I including too much information and overloading readers?
- Am I including too little information and omitting important facts and statistics?
- Is the tone appealing and respectful, or does it sound condescending?

- Are the statistics simple enough for readers to understand, yet complete enough for them to make reasoned choices?
- Are my sources credible and unbiased?
- What is the best way to explain complicated medical concepts when even scientists and physicians disagree?

Admittedly, the answers to these questions have more to do with choosing the right course of action than taking a moral or ethical stand. Still, it is up to each of us to make a personal commitment to communicate health information in ways that are clear, simple, honest, and complete.

Strategies, Ideas, and Suggestions

Readers. Learn as much as you can about your potential audience—in general, not specific. This means knowing about their familiarity with the subject matter as well as likely frame of mind when they read the document. Also, find out about their primary language, culture, and literacy level. (You can find adult literacy estimates by state, county, congressional district, and city or town at www.casas.org/lit/litcode/ Search.cfm).

Goals. Be clear about why you are writing this document and what you expect readers to know, do, and feel as a result of reading it. Use these goals to determine which is essential "need-to-know" information that must be included and what is "nice-to-know" background information that can be deleted.

When writing about diabetes, for example, need-to-know information may be about nutrition and exercise while nice-to-know information can be about physiology of the digestive process. Of course, some reference to physiology can help readers understand why exercise and proper nutrition are recommended.

Writing team. A team can help weigh choices and determine which information to include or omit. At a minimum, this team should include: subject-matter expert(s) (perhaps a scientist or clinician) who verifies content accuracy, a writer who advocates for plain language, and at least one reader who understands and represents the intended audience. The expert's and the reader's opinions are equally important. As a writer, your job is to balance content, word choice, and graphics to satisfy the needs of both.

Plain language and word choice. Using plain language means putting information into context with examples, stories, and analogies and formatting the document to be inviting and easy to read. It also means using words people already know and defining ones they must learn.

Sometimes, though, even "simple" words can cause problems. For example, the word "suggest" can easily be misinterpreted. Even though scientists know that the phrase "study data suggests" refers to preliminary data, lay readers may leap to the conclusion that the term indicates a higher level of proof. You can help by putting words like "may," "might," and "could" into context and clarifying terms that are potentially misunderstood. (To learn more, go to Plain Language on page 179.)

Numbers. Numbers, especially very large ones, can pose concerns because they are hard for most people to comprehend. When talking about statistics, for example, it's generally easier for people to understand "about 1 out of every 3 people" rather than "329 people out of 1,000." Since people often prefer percentages, you can add in parentheses (33%). It's important, though, not to misrepresent the statistics. Three people out of a study involving ten subjects can be said to represent 30 percent of the study. But that's not the same thing as 346 people out of 1000.

Carefully designed graphics such as tables or pie charts can also help make statistics clearer. One way to make sure tables are easy to read is by having just two or three columns of the most pertinent information. In addition, round-out numbers to no more than one decimal figure, such as "26.2" instead of "26.215."

References. Where information comes from is as important as how it is presented. Use the best data available to help readers make wise and informed decisions. This often means doing your own literature search, starting with articles in peer-reviewed journals. Once you are sure that data has been rigorously evaluated, supplement it with information found in "grey literature" (nonpeer-reviewed materials like magazines, newsletters, and conference proceedings), on websites, and from product materials.

Mandated materials. As a writer, your job is to present information that is both honest and complete without being overwhelming. This is a challenge, especially when you are working with medical-legal documents for which the language has been mandated. Examples include informed consent materials and government information like HIPAA regulations. If you cannot alter these documents, provide help to readers by writing easier-to-read summaries that you can attach. My dentist, for example, has a one-page summary of HIPAA information stapled on top of the more complex regulations he needs to hand out.

Uncertainty and ambiguity. Another potential concern is the fact that medical information is constantly changing and often even experts disagree about what is correct. For instance, should people eat a lot of high-fat protein foods or more low-fat grains? Ambiguity needs to be both acknowledged and addressed so your readers are not misled. One way do this is to preface information by stating that scientists continue to study and learn, letting readers know that what may seem correct today may change tomorrow.

In many ways, health professionals are translators of scientific and medical information—writing complicated, rapidly-changing, numbers-based information in a manner that is clear and simple enough for "average readers" to understand.

Sources to Learn More

Adult Literacy Estimates, available at
http://www.casas.org/lit/litcode/Search.cfm. Accessed January 19, 2004.

Bennett P, 1999. Communicating about risks to public health. *Centre for Environmental Research and Training*, England: University of Birmingham. Available at http://www.doh.gov.uk/pointers.htm. Accessed January 18, 2004.

Lipkus IM, Hollands JG, 1999. "The visual communication of risk," *Journal of the National Cancer Institute*, Monograph 25:149–163.

Ogden J et al., 2003. "What's in a name? An experimental study of patients' views of the impact and function of a diagnosis," *Family Practice*, 20(3):248–253.

Osborne H, 2004. "In other words...the ethics of simplicity," *On Call* magazine, 7(2):16–17. Available at http://www.healthliteracy.com. Accessed March 12, 2004. Information is adapted and reprinted with permission of *On Call* magazine. *On Call* is published by BostonWorks, a division of the *Boston Globe*.

Feedback: Interviews and Focus Groups

Starting Points

Regardless of the document you are creating, it is well worthwhile to ask for ongoing feedback from people who represent the intended reading audience. Whether you interview people one-to-one or meet with them in focus groups, audience feedback helps throughout the writing process.

When writing patient teaching sheets, for example, you can use feedback in the beginning of the project to determine the most important topics to include. As you write, you can use feedback to assess how clearly you are communicating key messages. And even when your project is complete, readers can give you feedback about what to change in the next revision.

As valuable as feedback is, it is an often overlooked and omitted step. In part, this may be because interviews and focus groups take time and cost money. It may also be that writers and committees are under deadline to get their newly written documents into use. And sometimes feedback doesn't happen because writers feel they already know the reader's perspective. This is seldom the case, however, because writers are so familiar with the content that they cannot judge if the words and concepts make sense to others. Also, writers are not the end-users of most materials and therefore cannot gauge personal relevance. Indeed, the true experts about written materials are the readers. An example from a consulting experience I had follows:

Several years ago, an administrator from a large medical center asked me to help revise the General Authorization Form they give to all patients. She told me that this document had been "stuck in committee" for a long time, as the doctors and lawyers couldn't agree on content and word choice.

In this revision, we asked for feedback from intended readers, including adult students in the medical center's English as a Second Language class and members of a local senior center. These readers told us that, although the words were clear and easy to read, they didn't understand some of the concepts. Many questioned, for example, what it means to "track medical devices." In response, we added a clearly written explanation of this term and asked for their feedback again. When the readers told us they understood, the administrators and lawyers were satisfied and approved the form.

Strategies, Ideas, and Suggestions

Know your intended audience. At the start of new projects, find out about the learning abilities, information needs, language, and culture of your intended audience. Beyond looking at demographics, meet with several potential readers and ask what types of information they require. For example, in addition to self-care instructions readers may be interested in how much a procedure costs or how often they will need follow-up appointments.

Ask early, ask often. Feedback is beneficial at all stages of the writing process. After you complete a first draft and are reasonably confident that your material is clear and easy to read, ask intended readers for their feedback. Once you make revisions based on their feedback, ask again to make sure you didn't introduce new problems. Continue this process until your readers confirm that they truly understand.

Interviews. Interviewing one person at a time is a flexible and effective way to get feedback. This technique can be particularly useful when asking for opinions from people who fear embarrassment (perhaps due to limited literacy), are unaccustomed to giving opinions in front of others, or lack the fluency needed to speak up.

Although interviews seem spontaneous, you should plan the questions to ask ahead of time. Frame them as open-ended queries such as "What do you like about the pictures in this booklet?" rather than yes/no questions like "Does this booklet look good to you?"

Also observe how people engage with your material. For example, notice whether people smile when looking at the illustrations or seem confused by the charts and graphs. Encourage interviewees to "think aloud" and to talk about their reactions as they read the entire document.

Focus groups. Focus groups are another effective way of getting feedback. Generally, groups have six to eight people who represent the intended audience in terms of age, literacy, language, culture, and familiarity with the subject matter. Most groups are co-led by a trained facilitator who asks questions and a recorder who takes notes.

Some people are more willing than others to participate in focus groups. Teenagers and college students, for example, are often very comfortable with this format as they are accustomed to giving opinions in classroom settings.

Interviews, focus groups, or both. Sometimes it's hard to know whether to ask for feedback in an interview, focus group, or perhaps both. Jeanne McGee's book, *Writing and Designing Print Materials for Beneficiaries: A Guide for State Medicaid Agencies* clearly outlines issues to consider when deciding which format to use (McGee, 1999).

Surveys. A survey or questionnaire that you attach to a document can serve as a hybrid between interviews and focus groups. With a survey, people can respond anonymously to specific feedback questions. To make it easier to complete, you might pose questions in a yes/no format. For example, "Do you think that people will want to read this booklet? __Yes __No" (To learn about writing surveys, go to Forms and Other "Reading-to-Do" Documents on page 67.)

Budgeting for feedback. Acquiring feedback does not always require a large budget or a lot of participants. In fact, a representative sample of just 10 to 20 people will likely tell you if anything is seriously wrong. Whatever your budget, try to arrange for at least two rounds of feedback testing. The first round is to identify areas you need to revise. The second round is to make sure you did not add new problems when you made these revisions.

Asking for opinions. When you ask people to review materials, make it clear that you are testing the material and not their reading or comprehension skills. Make sure you ask questions in ways that help people feel comfortable expressing opinions. Begin by asking, "Will you help me?" Then let people know how you will use their feedback and offer to show them updated versions. At the end of your interview or focus group, make sure to sincerely thank people for sharing their opinions.

Questions to ask. Determine in advance what areas you want to learn more about. Be reasonable in your expectations and appreciate that you cannot ask about everything. Instead, pick and choose the areas that you have the most questions about or are the most important. Here are examples of some feedback questions (adapted from Brandes, 1996):

- **Attractiveness.** "Can you tell me what you like (or don't like) about _____?"
- **Understandability.** "When it says _____ what does this mean to you?"
- **Personal relevance.** "Is _____ something you would be likely to do?"
- **Acceptability.** "Why do you think it is important for people to know about _____?"
- **Actions.** "Would you show me how you will do _____?"
- **Ease of use.** "Can I watch as you (follow these instructions) or (read this booklet)?"
- **Overall impressions.** "What, if anything, did we leave out that should be included?"

Regardless of the type of document you are creating, it is well worthwhile to ask for ongoing feedback from people who represent the intended reading audience.

Sources to Learn More

Brandes WL (ed.), 1996. *Literacy, Health, and the Law: An Exploration of the Law and the Plight of Marginal Reader Within the Healthcare System.* Philadelphia, PA: Health Promotion Council of Southeastern Pennsylvania, Inc.

National Cancer Institute, 1994. *Clear & Simple: Developing Effective Print Materials for Low-Literate Readers.* National Institutes of Health.

Doak CC, Doak LG, Root JH, 1996. *Teaching Patients with Low Literacy Skills,* 2nd ed. Philadelphia, PA: J.B. Lippincott Company.

Krueger RA, Casey MA, 2000. *Focus Groups: A Practical Guide for Applied Research,* 3rd ed. Thousand Oaks, CA: Sage Publications, Inc.

McGee J, 1999. *Writing and Designing Print Materials for Beneficiaries: A Guide for State Medicaid Agencies.* HCFA Publication Number 10145. Baltimore, MD: Centers for Medicare & Medicaid Services, U.S. Department of Health and Human Services. (A second edition is forthcoming in 2004. For ordering information, contact Jeanne McGee, McGee & Evers Consulting, Inc., Vancouver, Washington, 360-574-4744, jmcgee@pacifier.com).

_____, (anticipated publication, 2004). *How to Collect and Use Reactions From Readers to Improve Written Materials.* Baltimore, MD: Centers for Medicare & Medicaid Services, U.S. Department of Health and Human Services. (For ordering information, contact Jeanne McGee, McGee & Evers Consulting, Inc., Vancouver, Washington, 360-574-4744, jmcgee@pacifier.com).

Osborne H, 2001. "In other words... can they understand? Testing patient education materials with intended readers," *On Call* magazine, 4(11):26–27. Available at http://www.healthliteracy.com. Accessed January 19, 2004. Information is adapted and reprinted with permission of *On Call* magazine. *On Call* is published by BostonWorks, a division of the *Boston Globe.*

_____, 2000. *Overcoming Communication Barriers in Patient Education.* Gaithersburg, MD: Aspen Publishers, Inc.

Sudman S, Bradburn NM, 1982. *Asking Questions: A Practical Guide to Questionnaire Design.* San Francisco, CA.: Jossey-Bass, Inc.

Schriver KA, 1997. *Dynamics in Document Design.* New York, NY: John Wiley & Sons, Inc.

Feng Shui and Other Environmental Considerations

Starting Points

Patients and providers often discuss intimate healthcare matters such as life, death, and bodily functions. These very personal and often emotional conversations can be even more difficult when they take place in environments that feel cold and impersonal. Unfortunately, many healthcare institutions are like this with their florescent lighting, institutional-beige walls, built-in metal furniture, and small cubicles that are divided only by thin partitions or curtains.

Feng Shui, based on an ancient Chinese art, is a way to offset these negatives and create an environment that has a more positive effect on people. Even if you are skeptical of these principles (as I admit I first was), incorporating some elements of Feng Shui (described below) can help you create environments that feel warmer, more personal, and conducive to intimate healthcare conversations.

> Mary's small office feels institutional (which it is) with its concrete walls, built-in bookshelves, and bright overhead florescent lighting. Knowing that she has limited options to change this environment, Mary brought in a small table lamp for her desk. With its translucent shade, the lamp casts a big pool of warm light rather than a narrow fluorescent band focused on just one part of her desk.
>
> Mary immediately feels more energetic by having this lamp in her office. Patients agree, for when they meet Mary in her office they now seem more comfortable, open, and spontaneous. Indeed, by just adding this one lamp, people comment how home-like and comfy Mary's office is.
>
> —Linda Varone, RN of Feng Shui Sanctuary/Nurturing Spaces

Strategies, Ideas, and Suggestions

Lighting. Although not visible, florescent lights flicker on and off up to 60 times per second. To offset this, you can add lamps with incandescent bulbs or let in natural sunlight by opening window shades and blinds.

Color. Medical settings generally have little color, with mostly beige or light pastel walls. Clinicians, too, usually dress in white or light-colored uniforms and jackets. You can add a dose of color and visual interest by using wallpaper borders or decorative room accents like pillows or pictures. And, if your dress code permits, you may also want to wear a colorful pin or scarf on your lab coat or uniform.

Sound. There are many sounds you can't control in healthcare settings, such as overhead announcements, hallway conversations, and equipment being wheeled from one room to another. To counter these, consider playing soothing background music to filter out intrusive sounds.

Living things. People often feel more at ease when they are around living things like plants and animals. While there may be institutional restrictions on bringing in live plants or other living things, consider at least having a silk plant or small stuffed animal.

Movement. Often, little happens in corners. To create a sense of movement and add energy to these quiet spaces, think about adding a mobile, table-top water fountain, or pleasant-sounding wind chime.

Texture. Healthcare settings have a distinctive institutional feel to them, with many hard or cold surfaces like concrete walls and stainless steel furniture. To counteract these, you can introduce a softer throw pillow or fabric table cover.

Furniture. You can create settings that feel private and intimate even when there is built-in furniture and other fixtures you cannot change. You may, for example, want to use a moveable bookcase to create a sense of privacy. You can also position chairs and beds so that people can see out of doorways and are not surprised when someone enters the room.

Artwork. Personalize spaces by adding calming photographs or artwork. Chose items appropriate to the patients you are treating, such as pictures of older adults for a geriatric clinic. Since people's taste differ, have a variety of artwork so most everyone finds something to help them feel more at ease.

Clutter. Providers often have books, paperwork, and numerous health-related items scattered about. It can feel cluttered when these objects look messy or not cared for. Like all forms of communication, simplicity helps. Periodically clean out what you display (and also what you store) to give your space a feeling of openness and simplicity.

Accessibility. Beyond using Feng Shui, make sure your environment is accessible to everyone—including people with disabilities. Have handrails and straight-backed chairs for people with balance or movement problems, large-print and plain language signs and reading materials for people who have trouble seeing or reading, quiet and well-lit spaces for people with limited hearing, and soothing, simple wallpapers and artwork for people who may be distracted or easily upset. (To learn more, go to the Americans with Disabilities Act website at http://www.usdoj.gov/crt/ada/adahom1.htm.)

Even if you are skeptical of Feng Shui as I admit I first was, these principles can help you create environments that feel warmer, more personal, and conducive to intimate healthcare conversations.

Sources to Learn More

Americans with Disabilities Act, http://www.usdoj.gov/crt/ada/adahom1.htm. Accessed January 21, 2004.

Birdsall G, 1998. *The Feng Shui Companion.* Rochester, VT: Destiny Books.

Chin, RD, 1998. *Feng Shui Revealed.* New York: Clarkson Potter.

International Feng Shui Guild. Available at http://www.fengshuiguild.com. Accessed January 20, 2004.

Lazenby G, 1998. *The Feng Shui House Book.* New York: Watson-Guptill.

Mitchell S, 1998. *Tao Te Ching, A New English Version.* New York: Harper Collins Publishers.

Osborne H, 2001. "In other words...using Feng Shui to improve healthcare communication," *On Call* magazine, 4(5):46–47. Available at http://www.healthliteracy.com. Accessed January 20, 2004. Information is adapted and reprinted with permission of *On Call* magazine. *On Call* is published by BostonWorks, a division of the *Boston Globe.*

Rossbach S. 1987. *Interior Design with Feng Shui.* New York: E.P. Dutton.

Forms and Other "Reading-to-Do" Documents

Starting Points

Healthcare is filled with forms and other "reading-to-do" documents that require readers to perform tasks such as fill in insurance numbers, rate satisfaction, check off instruction boxes, and sign consent. To accomplish these tasks, readers must not only comprehend text but also locate, recall, and enter information from other parts of the document, from other materials, or from memory.

These are difficult tasks for many people to do. According to the United States National Adult Literacy Survey (NALS) and International Adult Literacy Survey (IALS), nearly one out of two adults has marginal literacy skills or less and has difficulty reading text as in newspapers and books. Even more people, especially older adults aged 65 and over, have trouble with documents like forms, charts, schedules, maps, and bills (Kirsch, et al. 1993; Brown, et al. 1996; Statistics Canada, 2000).

An example from a volunteer experience I had follows:

One reason that documents are so difficult is that they assume readers understand jargon and acronyms. But this assumption is often incorrect. For example, I was tutoring an Egyptian woman new to English and saw how baffled she was when a form asked for her PIN number. Unfamiliar with the acronym for "personal identification number," this woman wondered why she needed a safety pin to get an identification card.

Strategies, Ideas, and Suggestions

Know your audience. Know (generally, not specifically) about the people who will be using your form. This means knowing demographics including age, literacy level, and languages spoken. It also means learning whether the audience is likely to have physical or cognitive limitations that might impair their ability to see, comprehend, and remember. Be aware, as well, about your readers' fund of knowledge and make sure they are familiar with the types of information your form is asking for.

Limit your objectives. When writing forms and other reading-to-do documents, ask people only for the information you need now or will need very soon. For example, don't ask people for their children's names and ages just because you'll need this data sometime later. Instead, ask only when you truly need to know.

Write in a friendly tone. Let readers know at the beginning of your document why you need certain information. For example, start with "We take pride in patient care at MNO Medical Center. Please fill out this short survey and let us know how well we are doing." Use a conversational tone throughout, referring to readers as "you" and the organization as "we." Don't get bogged down, however, with too many pleasantries. Sometimes an abundance of "please" and "thank you" statements obscures the form's intent. At the end, thank readers for completing the survey and, as with all written materials, include a way to get more information.

Consistent wording. Be consistent in your wording and make sure that the labels, questions, and instructions ("given information") on your document exactly match its items and answers ("requested information"). Do not, for example, say "Age Group" in one place and "How old are you?" in another. Instead, you might keep the first heading and then ask, "What is your age?"

Tasks. Reading-to-do documents ask readers to take actions or to do tasks. Here are some ways to make these tasks clear and easy for readers:

- Show, do not just tell, how to take the needed actions. For example, show an answer that is correctly circled rather than underlined, or a date written as mm/dd/yyyy.

- Suggest that readers circle words they do not know and have staff available to explain what these words mean.

- Ask for concrete information such as name, date, time, or place rather than abstract information such as how/why or cause/effect.

- Be specific in your instructions, such as stating whether to "check one box" or "check all that apply."

- Ask for information in a consistent way. For example, ask people only for yes/no responses and not also to fill-in-the-blank and rate items on a scale from 1–5.

- Let readers know the sections they need to complete and those they can skip. You can do this by following a yes/no response with "If no, go to section (x)".

- Line up the numbers in rows and columns (rather than writing about them in full sentences) when asking people to do math calculations.

Ease of use. Make sure your documents are easy for readers to see and complete. This means having 12-point font or larger, sufficiently large spaces for people to write their answers, and generous white space so the print doesn't look crowded. Don't squeeze everything onto one page when two are really needed.

Show, do not just tell. This is particularly important with concepts that people have trouble with such as estimating distances, dimensions, and weights. Figure 1.1 not only helps people understand weights but also gives people like me (who are not good with the metric system) a visual tool as an aid.

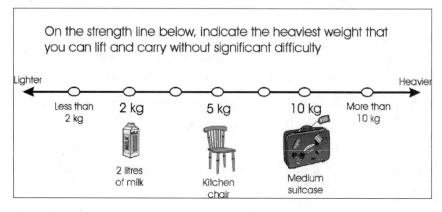

Figure 1.1. A visual example helps people understand concepts. *Source: Reprinted and used with permission of Michel Gauthier and Julian Evetts.*

Environment. Help people relax and focus on your document by providing a comfortable environment in which they have sufficient time to read, adequate lighting to see, and can ask for help when they need it. Encourage staff to offer assistance to patients who ask or seem to have difficulty. You can do this respectfully by saying, "Many people find these forms hard to fill out. Would you like me to help you?"

Test your document. Make sure your documents are not only readable but also usable. Assume the role of the reader and ask yourself, "Is this difficult reading?" and "How complex is the task that readers are being asked to do?" Try the form yourself and make sure you can complete it within the given time, in the appropriate space, and with the needed information.

After you are satisfied, test the form with intended readers. Notice where they have difficulty and ask for suggestions about how to improve the form. Take readers' feedback seriously and use their suggestions to make needed changes. (To learn more about feedback, go to Feedback: Interviews and Focus Groups on page 57.)

Healthcare is filled with forms and other "reading-to-do" documents that require readers to complete tasks such as fill in insurance numbers, rate satisfaction, check off instruction boxes, and sign consent.

Sources to Learn More

American Medical Association Foundation and the American Medical Association, 2003. *Health literacy: Help your patients understand.* Available at http://www.ama-assn.org/ama/pub/category/9913.html. Accessed January 22, 2004.

Brown H, Prisuta R, Jacobs B, Campbell A, 1996. *Literacy of Older Adults in America.* National Center for Education Statistics. Washington, D.C.: U.S. Department of Education.

Communication Canada, 2003. *Successful Communication Tool Kit.* Available online at http://www.communication.gc.ca/services/alpha_lit/2003/scr2003_toc.html. Accessed January 20, 2004.

Doak CC, Doak LG, Root JH, 1996. *Teaching Patients with Low Literacy Skills,* 2nd ed. Philadelphia, PA: J.B. Lippincott Company.

Gauthier M, Evetts J, Mosenthal P, Kirsch I, 2003. *Literacy Task Analysis Guide.* Human Resources Development Canada. Available online at http://www.ibd.ab.ca/Literacy-task.html. Accessed January 20, 2004.

Kirsch I, Jungeblut A, Jenkins L, Kolstad A, 1993. *Adult Literacy in America.* Washington, D.C.: National Center for Education Statistics.

National Literacy and Health Program, 1998. *Creating Plain Language Forms for Seniors: A Guide for the Public, Private, and Not-for-Profit Sectors.* Canadian Public Health Association. Available at http://www.nlhp.cpha.ca/publications.htm. Accessed January 20, 2004.

Osborne H, 2003. "In other words…make it easy … writing healthcare forms that patients can understand and complete," *On Call* magazine, 6(3):16–17. Available at http://www.healthliteracy.com. Accessed January 20, 2004. Information is adapted and reprinted with permission of *On Call* magazine. *On Call* is published by BostonWorks, a division of the *Boston Globe.*

———, 1999. "In other words…creating medical forms people can understand," *On Call* magazine, 2(5):46–47 Available at http://www.healthliteracy.com. Accessed January 20, 2004.

Health Canada, 1999. *Communicating with Seniors: Advice, Techniques and Tips.* Ottawa, Ontario: Minster of Health. Available online at www.hc-sc.gc.ca/seniors-aines/pubs/communicating/pdf/comsen_e.pdf. Accessed January 20, 2004.

Statistics Canada, 2000. *Literacy in the information age: Final report of the international adult literacy survey.* Available online at http://www.statcan.ca/start.html. Accessed January 20, 2004.

Groups, Classes, and Educational Programs

Starting Points

Groups, classes, and other educational programs are excellent ways to communicate health information. These types of learning experiences generally combine formal teaching with informal discussion and group interaction. This way, participants (or "members" or "students") not only can learn from the group's leaders (or "facilitators" or "teachers") but also gain knowledge and support from each other.

Though similar—groups, classes, and educational programs differ in important ways. Groups tend to be fairly informal, with built-in flexibility to accommodate participants' specific needs and interests. Self-help and support groups (in-person or online) fall into this category. Classes are often more structured with a formal curriculum and clear-cut goals. Classes may focus on specific topics such as diseases and medical procedures or on more general themes like wellness and health promotion. Educational programs are a hybrid of both groups and classes, offering a standardized curriculum with many opportunities for support and interaction. An example follows:

> The "COPD Program" is designed to teach patients diagnosed with chronic obstructive pulmonary disease (COPD) how to cope with their disease on a day-to-day basis. It successfully brings people together who would otherwise be isolated, benefiting participants on a very practical and personal level. "George," for instance, was newly diagnosed with COPD but was already in the end stages of the disease. He struggled with almost every self-care task, including taking a shower. When he mentioned this, another program participant told him step-by-step how she shampoos her hair without getting symptomatic. Hearing this from someone who lives with COPD, George gained the confidence and know-how to cope with at least one of his daily challenges.

Strategies, Ideas, and Suggestions

Leadership. Effective leaders are more than just subject matter experts. They should be enthusiastic about teaching and enjoy helping people learn. Beyond good teaching skills, leaders should enjoy public speaking, be flexible, and have a sense of humor. These extra skills come in handy when the unplanned happens—which it invariably does.

Leadership should match each program's specific needs. For example, health classes are usually taught by medical professionals who are experts on a particular topic. Support groups may be led by peers who have first-hand experience with the subject matter. Educational programs may be co-led by patients or community members and providers who, together, share responsibility for leadership and teaching.

Privacy and confidentiality. Whether your group meets in-person or takes place in cyberspace, make sure that it feels safe and is private. This means establishing clear ground rules at the beginning about privacy and confidentiality. You may want people to sign a statement acknowledging these rules and agreeing to follow them.

Environment. For in-person meetings, select a facility with ample parking and that, ideally, is close to public transportation. Make sure the facility is also accessible to people with disabilities. Choose comfortable meeting rooms that have adequate lighting, easy access to the temperature controls, and are close to bathrooms and emergency exits.

When meeting in cyberspace (such as Internet chat groups) you can create a welcoming and safe environment by alerting participants to privacy policies, letting everyone know the discussion ground rules, and designing the associated website so that it is accessible to people with disabilities. To learn more about designing accessible websites, go to Website Design on page 251.

Goals. Be clear about goals—what participants will know, do, and feel as a result of joining your group, class, or educational program. Design a curriculum with these goals in mind and offer a variety of ways to accomplish them. For example, use a combination of teaching strategies like lectures, handouts, discussions, and practical exercises to engage people—both students and teachers—who understand best by seeing, hearing, or doing. Additionally, handouts and other written materials not only are helpful during class time but also give participants something tangible to review later.

Teaching adults. Incorporate the principles of adult learning into your teaching. Principles include that:

1) adults are motivated to learn as they experience needs and interests that learning will satisfy
2) adults' orientation to learning is life-centered
3) experience is the richest resource for adults' learning
4) adults have a deep need to be self-directing
5) individual differences among people increase with age (Knowles, 1990)

In practical terms, teaching adults means being flexible. You might begin sessions by asking participants about the topics they want to focus on that day. If possible, modify the agenda to address these topics while staying true to the core curriculum. Then include plenty of opportunities for interaction and questions. At the end, conclude with a summary and ask participants about the actions they plan to take.

Scheduling. Sometimes the hardest part of running a session is finding a convenient meeting time and place. Consider not only your workload and the facility's room availability but also take into account the rhythms and routines of potential group members. This means finding out whether participants are more likely to attend weekday meetings or can only come in the evening or on weekends. Give thought, as well, to upcoming holidays, public transportation schedules, and even the weather.

Participants. Appreciate that not all participants are equally motivated. Some people may be reluctant to join groups or classes, enrolling only because their provider or family member encourages them to do so. Allow participants to learn at their own pace. Over time, many leaders have found that even the most reluctant participants become active group members once they experience the many benefits of being with others who share common interests.

Marketing, promotion, and referrals. Make it easy for people to learn about, register for, and refer others to your program. This generally means marketing to the general public, promoting your program directly to likely participants, and keeping referral sources (like primary care providers) well aware of the services you offer. Here are some ways:

- Let the community at large know about your program through announcements in the newspaper, on television and radio, and even in newsletters and bulletins of local organizations. You might also want to list the program and registration information on your facility's website.

- As your facility allows, get the word out to patients and families through "in-house" methods such as brochures, posters, and notices in exam rooms, waiting rooms, lobbies, and even elevators.

- Inform primary care providers and other referral sources about your teaching programs and highlight how these sessions can improve patient care. As appropriate and in keeping with privacy policies, let providers know when their patients enroll and if there are significant problems or successes.

- Regardless of how you promote your program, highlight its benefits from the perspective of participants. One way to do this is to include a few quotes (with permission, of course) from satisfied attendees.

Evaluation and feedback. Make sure your program meets the needs of its participants. You can do this by soliciting feedback informally and formally. Informally, ask participants what they want to learn more about and then use their suggestions in your next session. Use a formal evaluation tool to measure success by asking specific questions about the program's content and format. Whether you ask for feedback formally or informally, allow opportunities for participants to tell you—in their own words—about their experience with your group program.

Appreciate that not all participants are equally motivated. Some people may be reluctant to participate in a group or class, enrolling only because their provider or family member encourages them to do so.

Sources to Learn More

Chronic disease self-management program, Stamford School of Medicine. Available at http://patienteducation.stanford.edu/programs. Accessed January 21, 2004.

Frank, et al., 1995. Alliance not compliance: A philosophy of outpatient care, *Journal of Clinical Psychiatry*, 56 (suppl 1):11–17.

Funnell MM, Anderson RM, 1999. "Putting humpty dumpty back together again: Reintegrating the clinical and behavioral components in diabetes care and education," *Diabetes Spectrum*, 12(1):19–24.

Knowles M, 1990. *The Adult Learner: A Neglected Species*, 4th ed. Houston, TX: Gulf Publishing Company.

Lorig KR, et al., 1999. "Evidence suggesting that a chronic disease self-management program can improve health status while reducing hospitalization," *Medical Care*, 37(1):5–4.

Osborne H, 2002a. *Partnering with Patients To Improve Health Outcomes*. Gaithersburg, MD: Aspen Publishers, Inc. Information is adapted and reprinted with the author's permission.

_____, 2002b. "In other words…getting formal…educating patients in a classroom setting," *On Call* magazine, 5(6):30–31. Available at http://www.healthliteracy.com. Accessed January 22, 2004. Information is adapted and reprinted with permission of *On Call* magazine. *On Call* is published by BostonWorks, a division of the *Boston Globe*.

Redman BK, 1993. *The Process of Patient Education*, 7th ed. St. Louis, MO: Mosby Year Book.

Wellington M, 2001. "Stanford health partners: Rationale and early experiences in establishing physician group visits and chronic disease self-management workshops," *J Ambulatory Care Management*, 24(3):10–16.

Hearing: Communicating with People Who Are Deaf or Hard of Hearing

Starting Points

Many people have hearing impairments that range from mild losses of sensitivity to total hearing loss. People who are deaf from birth often identify themselves as Deaf (with an upper-case "D") to indicate they are part of a specific cultural and linguistic community.

More commonly, people lose hearing as they age. In fact, according to the American Speech-Language-Hearing Association, more than one-half of all people aged 65 and older have some form of hearing loss.

Whether Deaf or hard of hearing, people with hearing impairments need to communicate in ways other than just talking and listening. Many Deaf people use American Sign Language (ASL). More than simply hand gestures that substitute for spoken English, ASL is a complex language with its own grammar and syntax that makes use of facial expressions, body movements, and hand signs. Other strategies that people may use include reading lips, communicating in writing, or using assistive listening devices such as hearing aids and telephone amplification systems. These methods are more than just a courtesy. In fact, the 1990 United States Americans with Disabilities Act (ADA) requires that public facilities, including hospitals and health centers, communicate in ways that people with hearing impairments can understand.

Alice, who is hard of hearing, just started going to a new dental office. She lets the staff know that she has a progressive hearing loss and wears a hearing aid. Betty, the dental hygienist, assumes Alice's hearing aid adequately compensates for her hearing loss and so continues to communicate with Alice as she does with other patients. They speak only briefly before Betty puts on her mask to clean Alice's teeth. This is a problem, however, as Alice can only hear Betty's voice but not distinguish her words.

Six months later, Alice has an appointment with a new hygienist, Cindy. Cindy turns off the radio in the office and sits down to talk with Alice. They discuss what will happen during the cleaning procedure and, together, figure out how to communicate when Cindy wears her mask. Needless to say, Alice feels more positive about this appointment and understands the information that Cindy is communicating.

Strategies, Ideas, and Suggestions

Determine the preferred method for communicating. Ask Deaf patients and those who are hard of hearing how they prefer to communicate. This may be moving your chair to face patients directly so they can see your lips, communicating in writing, or using an ASL interpreter. Find out also whether patients use assistive listening devices and if they have a TTY (telephone typewriter) where they live or work.

Environment. Meet in a quiet space that is free of distracting noises such as air conditioners or overhead pages. Look for a space that has adequate lighting so that the other person can clearly see you when you talk. As appropriate, tap people lightly on their shoulders to get their attention and to orient them to where the sound is coming from. When you need to get someone's attention in a large waiting area, go up to that person directly rather than just using the public address system. You can also create an environment that feels welcoming by using basic sign language phrases and greetings.

Articulate clearly. Speak distinctly, not necessarily loudly. Shouting is unpleasant and not helpful as it distorts mouth movements and makes lip reading more difficult. Shouting may also interfere with a hearing aid's ability to pick up usable sounds. Instead, use a slower rate of speech but don't exaggerate pronunciation to the point that you distort individual words.

Lip reading. People lip-read when they look at someone's mouth and speech-read when they also look at the other person's gestures, expressions, and pantomime actions. Sometimes messages are misinterpreted because pairs of words look alike such as "bed" and "men," or "pain" and "main."

Hearing

People who rely on visual cues may have particular difficulty understanding someone who has a mustache or speaks with an accent. To improve understanding, do not cover your mouth, chew gum, or talk at the same time as someone else.

Written notes don't always work. It is widely assumed that all people with hearing losses benefit from written information. But this is not necessarily so—particularly for those who have been deaf since birth and, despite normal intelligence, may read only at a fourth- to fifth-grade level. One reason for this lower reading level is that those who have never heard speech cannot "sound out" words—a technique that hearing people commonly use to figure out unfamiliar words. Rather than assume that written notes will help, ask the other person about the best way to communicate.

Electronic devices and equipment. Familiarize yourself with a TTY (telephone typewriter), a device that allows people with hearing or speech loss to communicate by telephone. This communication is facilitated through the telephone company's phone relay system that, at no charge, transmits messages between a TTY and standard telephone. To learn more, contact your local phone company.

ASL interpreters. When communicating with people who use ASL, ask to work with trained interpreters. Despite good intentions, untrained family members or friends who volunteer to interpret may not be skilled at communicating medical information and may also bring confidentiality and privacy concerns.

With a trained interpreter, start by making sure the patient is comfortable with the interpreter and familiar with the specific sign language being used. (ASL is not the only sign language.) Throughout the session, speak directly to the patient and not the interpreter. Position yourself so that the interpreter sits a little behind you and to the side. This way, the patient can see you and the interpreter in the same visual field. You, in turn, can listen to the interpreter while looking directly at the patient. You can find a database of interpreters for the Deaf at http://www.rid.org.

Technology and interpreters. Thanks to technology, patients, providers, and interpreters do not always have to be in the same room. One option is a video relay service that uses a high-speed Internet connection. This allows an interpreter, patient, and clinician to communicate from three separate locations. As yet, this technology is not perfect but still is better than no interpreter at all. To see a video sample, go to http://www.urmc.rochester.edu/strongconnections/.

Confirm Understanding. As with all types of health communication, take time to confirm understanding. Whether communicating directly or through an interpreter, ask Deaf and hard of hearing patients to tell you, in their own words, their understanding of the topics discussed. If a concept is unclear, rephrase it, don't just repeat it. And confirm understanding throughout your time together, not just when appointments are almost over.

More than simply hand gestures that substitute for spoken English, ASL is a complex language with its own grammar and syntax that makes use of facial expressions, body movements, and hand signs.

Sources to Learn More

American Speech-Language-Hearing Association. Available at http://www.asha.org/default.htm. Accessed January 21, 2004.

Americans with Disabilities Act, http://www.usdoj.gov/crt/ada/adahom1.htm. Accessed January 21, 2004.

Barnett S, 2002a. "Cross-cultural communication with patients who use American Sign Language," *Family Medicine*, 34(5):376–382.

_____, 2002b. "Communication with Deaf and hard-of-hearing people: A guide for medical education," *Academic Medicine*, 77(7):694–700.

_____, 1999. "Clinical and cultural issues in caring for Deaf people," *Family Medicine*, 31(1):17–22.

Hearing

D.E.A.F., Inc. (year unavailable). *Hearing Loss Awareness Kit.* Allston, MA: D.E.A.F., Inc. Available at http://www.deafinconline.org. Accessed January 21, 2004.

_____, (year unavailable). *Working with Deaf and Hard of Hearing Patients: A Guide for Medical Professionals.* Allston, MA: D.E.A.F., Inc.

National Institute of Arthritis and Musculoskeletal and Skin Diseases, 1995. *A Guide for Making Print Documents Accessible to Persons with Disabilities.* National Institutes of Health.

Osborne H, 2003. "In other words...communicating about health with ASL," *On Call* magazine, 6(6):16–17. Available at http://www.healthliteracy.com. Accessed January 22, 2004. Information is adapted and reprinted with permission of *On Call* magazine. *On Call* is published by BostonWorks, a division of the *Boston Globe.*

_____, 2002. *Partnering with Patients To Improve Health Outcomes.* Gaithersburg, MD: Aspen Publishers, Inc. Information is adapted and reprinted with the author's permission.

_____, 2000. *Overcoming Communication Barriers in Patient Education.* Gaithersburg, MD: Aspen Publishers, Inc. Information is adapted and reprinted with the author's permission.

Registry of Interpreters for the Deaf. Available at http://www.rid.org. Accessed January 22, 2004.

Strong Connections, TeleHealth Sing Language Solutions, University of Rochester. Available at http://www.urmc.rochester.edu/strongconnections/. Accessed January 21, 2004.

Helping Patients Prepare for and Participate in Healthcare

Starting Points

In today's busy world of healthcare, patients, their families, and caregivers assume ever-greater amounts of responsibility for treatment and care. In part, this increased responsibility comes from economic pressures that result in brief appointments and short hospitalizations. But it is also due to advances in technology and science which make it possible for people to monitor their symptoms and to use complex medical devices at home. Also, many patients (especially those of the younger generation) are savvy and informed consumers who want, and indeed expect, to fully participate in all aspects of health-related discussions, decisions, and directions.

From recognizing the first signs of medical problems to making end-of-life decisions, patients have responsibilities throughout the continuum of care. Health providers can help by educating patients about ways to prepare for and participate in these responsibilities. In offices, hospitals, homecare, and all situations in which health information is communicated, it is the provider's job to help patients be experts at being patients.

When Joan was diagnosed with colon cancer, she and her husband Eric opted to be involved in all aspects of her treatment and care. They did so while recognizing the limits of their knowledge and the importance of maintaining respectful relationships with their health providers.

Joan and Eric participated by searching the lay and professional literature, speaking with numerous specialists, and exploring tested and experimental treatment options. Before medical appointments, Joan and Eric even emailed their providers with questions they wanted to discuss. While this active level of participation certainly wasn't easy and definitely not fun, Joan and Eric felt good knowing that they were truly partners with her healthcare providers.

Strategies, Ideas, and Suggestions

Describe symptoms. Encourage patients to keep written records of their symptoms including when symptoms start, how often they occur, the length of time episodes last, and (as appropriate) what the symptoms look like. Help patients find ways to describe severity. Pain, for example, can be described numerically on scales from 1 to 10. It can also be expressed in words like "achy," "burning," "stabbing," "stiff," "tingly," "sore," and "annoying."

Keep personal health records. Suggest that patients, like providers, keep records of important health information. This way, patients can quickly and easily find what they need to know. You can help by suggesting they create notebooks with tabbed sections for:

- Medical problems
- Medications including prescription, over-the-counter medications, herbal remedies, and vitamins
- Health instructions
- Immunizations
- Test results
- Insurance information
- Contact information for family members or close friends
- Questions to ask
- Resources to learn more

Beyond clinical information, some patients and families find it helpful to assemble a notebook with more subjective and anecdotal health information. For example, the parents of an adult daughter who is non-verbal and diagnosed with autism created a 30-page notebook about her. They included comments and observations from their daughter's teachers and caregivers, with photos showing her capabilities. This notebook serves as a "living biography" that the family uses to introduce their daughter to new providers and caregivers.

Prepare for appointments. Help patients get the most from appointments by encouraging them to plan ahead of time what (and who) to bring. This means wearing needed devices like hearing aids or eyeglasses. It may also mean bringing all their medications (including prescriptions, over-the-counter, and home remedies) to appointments. And, especially when discussing diagnosis or treatment, encourage patients to bring a family member or trusted friend who can help listen, ask questions, and remember.

Ask questions. Many people have trouble thinking "on the spot," especially during medical appointments. Encourage patients to anticipate the questions they want to ask. Providers can help by giving patients tools like notepads (similar to a grocery lists) where they can write their questions and then take notes about diagnosis, tests, results, treatment, and other questions. See Figure 1.1 on the next page.

During appointments, pause periodically and ask patients for their questions. Be sensitive, however, to the fact that not everyone will speak up. Some people may find it hard to be "fully present" when they are in an examining room in an examining gown, and can only think of questions to ask when they are back at home. Others, like my mother, were taught that it is rude to question people in authority (like health professionals) and never feel comfortable doing so.

Start with the patient's experience. Patients are experts on what it's like to live with their disease or condition. Find out how much information patients want to know and how willing they are to be involved in treatment and care. Decide together what to discuss. You most likely can accommodate both their priorities and yours, but perhaps in a different order than you expected.

Media and direct-to-consumer information. Patients today may come to appointments already somewhat informed; they may have heard or read about their illnesses or medications in the newspaper, on television, via the Internet, or from direct-to-consumer advertising. Let patients know that you value their efforts and are open to their suggestions and questions. But also discuss the fact that sometimes information like this is incorrect, biased, or sensationalized.

Contact the office. Make it easy for patients to know how and when to contact you. Give them ways to reach your office (by

---

QRS Health Center Notepad

Here are some questions I want to ask my health provider.

_ **Diagnosis.** What is wrong with me? What causes it? How serious is it?

_____

_____

_ **Tests.** What tests do I need? Why do I need these tests?

_____

_____

_ **Results.** How do I find out about my test results? Will I be told if something is

okay or only if I need treatment?

_____

_____

_ **Treatment.** What treatment do I need? What choices do I have? What do I need to

do?

_____

_____

_ **Other questions.** Here is what else I want to know:

_____

_____

Figure 1.1. A notepad can help patients ask questions. Source: Helen Osborne, Health Literacy Consulting.

phone, email, or both) during business and non-business hours. Make sure to also let patients know where to go and what to do in emergency situations.

Sometimes, you may want to give patients or families additional ways to reach you—such as your direct pager or cell phone number.

Families, especially those caring for a very sick or dying patient at home, may be comforted by knowing how to reach "their provider" in an emergency. When you give contact information like this, however, make the conditions clear when people can contact you directly.

Confirm that you and your patients understand each other. Pause periodically (after key points and again at the end of appointments or conversations) and ask patients to tell you, in their own words, what you just talked about. Assume responsibility for understanding by starting with a statement like "I just want to make sure I explained this clearly. Please tell me how you will... ."

Help patients learn more. Make it easy for patients to learn as much as they want to know. Prepare lists of credible resources including books, articles, websites, hot lines, and associations. You might also want to let patients know about websites with tips to be more active patients. Well-regarded ones include http://www. Askme3.com, http://www.besttreatments.org, and http://www. mercksource. com.

In offices, hospitals, homecare, and all situations in which health information is communicated, it is the provider's job to help patients be experts at being patients.

Sources to Learn More

American Medical Association Foundation and the American Medical Association, 2003. *Health literacy: Help your patients understand.* Available at http://www.ama-assn.org/ama/pub/category/9913.html. Accessed January 22, 2004.

Ask Me 3. Available at http://www.askme3.com. Accessed January 22, 2004.

Best Treatments. "Includes information for patients and doctors about evidence-based medicine, shared decision-making, and risk," *BMJ*. Available at http://www.besttreatments.org. Accessed January 18, 2004.

Dickinson D, Raynor, 2003. "Ask the patients—they may want to know more than you think," *BMJ*, 327:861.

Ellner A, Hoey A, Frisch L, 2003. "Speak up! Can patients get better at working with their doctors?," *BMJ*, 327:303–304.

Funnell MM, Anderson RM, 1999. "Putting Humpty Dumpty back together again: Reintegrating the clinical and behavioral components in diabetes care and education," *Diabetes Spectrum*, 12(1):19–24.

Funnell MM, 2000. "Helping patients take charge of their chronic illnesses," *Family Practice Management*, 7(3):47–52.

Mercksource.com. Available at http://www.mercksource.com. Accessed February 19, 2004.

Osborne H, 2002. "In other words...from another point of view ... a patient's perspective about health communication," *On Call* magazine, 5(3):30–31. Available at http://www.healthliteracy.com. Accessed January 22, 2004. Information is adapted and reprinted with permission of *On Call* magazine. *On Call* is published by BostonWorks, a division of the *Boston Globe*.

_____, 2002. *Partnering with Patients To Improve Health Outcomes.* Gaithersburg, MD: Aspen Publishers, Inc. Information is adapted and reprinted with the author's permission.

Helping Patients Remember and Follow Medical Instructions

Starting Points

Correctly following medical instructions is difficult for many people. Studies show that 40–80% of the medical information that healthcare practitioners provide is immediately forgotten by patients (Kessels,

2003). Other studies find that 20–80% of patients make errors in taking medication and that 20–60% stop taking medications before being instructed to do so (Gottlieb, 2000).

These statistics are alarming, especially with all the healthcare responsibility that patients, families, and caregivers assume. A person with diabetes, for example, needs to fully understand what to do and be aware of when making numerous health decisions each day.

Whether about self-care procedures, medications, or needed behavioral and lifestyle changes, medical instructions are often hard for patients and caregivers to learn, remember, and follow. This is in part because the instructions may be complicated and explained in unfamiliar words and with lots of numbers. As well, people may have limited literacy or language skills, cognitive changes, or other learning barriers. Also, when patients are overwhelmed with new diagnoses or are scared, sick, or in pain, they may not be at their learning best.

Marian was 75-years-old when she suddenly went from being very healthy to being very sick. In just a week, she was diagnosed with two life-threatening illnesses, prescribed 22 medications, and asked to make appointments with numerous medical specialists. At times, Marian and her family said it felt like being in a foreign country with a new language like "therapeutic equivalents" and a new culture that was often rushed and impersonal.

One of the hardest tasks they faced was keeping track of Marian's many new medications. To help, her daughter-in-law created a visual guide (similar to a workplace training tool) to identify medications and note special instructions or questions. Using this guide, Marian and her family felt more comfortable and knowledgeable managing her medication and navigating their way through the healthcare system.

—From Mary Schutten (Marian's daughter-in law)
who created *Identimed*.

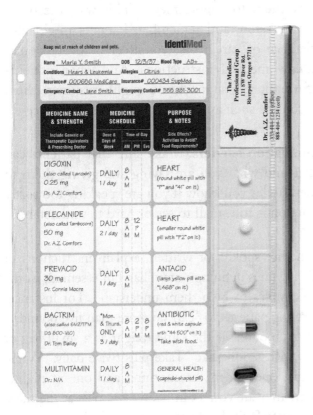

Figure 1.1. IdentiMed, a visual guide for managing multiple medications. Source: Reprinted with permission from Mary Schutten. To learn more about IdentiMed, go to http://www.identimed.com.

Strategies, Ideas, and Suggestions

Treatment plans. Medical instructions are especially hard to follow when patients have to change life-long habits and behaviors. To make this task easier, collaborate with patients to determine treatment plans they can and will adhere to. One way is to discuss the benefits of needed lifestyle changes. Periodically assess how well patients are following their treatment plans and then acknowledge their attempts as well as successes.

People. Many patients benefit by help from others. You might suggest, for example, that patients invite a family member or trusted friend to accompany them to appointments. This way, the other person can help learn, listen, and remember. Patients might also appreciate the assistance of caregivers (volunteer or professional) who help them follow medical instructions. And when patients need additional information or support, you might encourage them to talk with local resources such as a pharmacist or senior center.

Overcome communication barriers. Make sure that patients can hear, see, and understand what you are saying and giving them to read. Encourage them to let you know if you are speaking too softly or if printed information is too small to see or hard to understand.

Plain language. Whether spoken or written, explain instructions in plain language. This includes defining unfamiliar, but essential, words and giving people examples to help them understand. For instance, instead of just instructing patients to "Lift no more than five pounds," let them know that five pounds is the same weight as a small bag of flour. As well, clarify instructions like "Take pills twice daily." While you might mean "take one pill in the morning and one at night," patients might assume they are correct in taking two pills at the same time. (To learn more, go to Plain Language on page 179.)

Giving instructions.

- Link instructions to people's goals and values, such as how exercise can help them get strong enough to lift their young grandchildren.

- Give directions in sequence such as, "Do A, B, and then C" rather than in a more haphazard way like, "Before you do A, make sure to do D."

- Help people to identify what is most important by encouraging them to take notes or mark printed instructions with highlighters, "sticky" notes, arrows, or asterisks.

- Don't overwhelm patients with too much information. Focus on immediate skills and behaviors. When the time is right and they want to know, tell them more.

Adherence aids and reminders. Sometimes, people simply forget what to do. You might suggest they use pill boxes or similar adherence aids to help them remember when to take medication, or call patients to remind them of upcoming appointments. You can also create log sheets or similar tools which patients can check-off each time they complete a step or task. Also, encourage patients to come up with their own reminders such as a mnemonic (a word-based tool, similar to an acronym) or handwritten note to jog their memory.

Confirm understanding. As with all health communication, make sure that patients and their caregivers accurately understand. Assume responsibility by saying something like, "I just want to make sure I explained this clearly." Then ask people to tell you, in their own words, the instructions they agree to follow.

Ways to learn more. Help people learn as much as they want to know. Provide them with resources to contact when they have questions and concerns. Resources should not only include your office but also associations, support groups (local or virtual), websites, books, tapes, and consumer health libraries.

Whether about self-care procedures, medications, or needed behavioral and lifestyle changes, medical instructions are often hard for patients and caregivers to learn, remember, and follow.

Sources to Learn More

American Medical Association Foundation and the American Medical Association, 2003. *Health literacy: Help your patients understand.* Available at http://www.ama-assn.org/ama/pub/category/9913.html. Accessed January, 22, 2004.

Caregiving: Helping the elderly with activity limitations, 2000. *National Academy on an Aging Society.* No.7.

Drug Information Online at http://www.drugs.com. Accessed February 19, 2004.

Ellner A, Hoey A, Frisch L, 2003. "Speak up! Can patients get better at working with their doctors?," *BMJ*, 327:303–304.

Funnell MM, 2000. "Helping patients take charge of their chronic illnesses," *Family Practice Management*, 7(3):47–52.

Funnell MM, Anderson RM, 1999. "Putting Humpty Dumpty back together again: Reintegrating the clinical and behavioral components in diabetes care and education," *Diabetes Spectrum*, 12(1):19–24.

Gottlieb H, 2000. "Medication nonadherence: Finding solutions to a costly medical problem," *Drug Benefits Trends*, 12(6):57–62.

Identimed. Available at http://www.identimed.com. Accessed January 23, 2004.

Institute of Medicine, 2000. *To Err is Human: Building a Safer Health System.* Washington, D.C.: National Academy Press.

Kessels RPC, 2003. "Patients' memory for medical information," *Journal of the Royal Society of Medicine*, 96:219–222.

National Literacy and Health Program, 1998. *Working with Low-literacy Seniors: Practical Strategies for Health Providers.* Ontario, Canada: Canadian Public Health Association.

Osborne H, 2002a. "In other words...from another point of view...a patient's perspective about health communication," *On Call* magazine, 5(3):30–31. Available at http://www.healthliteracy.com. Accessed January 22, 2004. Information is adapted and reprinted with permission of *On Call* magazine. *On Call* is published by BostonWorks, a division of the *Boston Globe*.

———, 2002b. *Partnering with Patients To Improve Health Outcomes.* Gaithersburg, MD: Aspen Publishers, Inc. Information is adapted and reprinted with the author's permission.

———, 2001. "In other words...for their health...communicating with patients who have a chronic illness," *On Call* magazine, 4(12):26–27. Available at http://www.healthliteracy.com. Accessed January 22, 2004. Information is adapted and reprinted with permission of *On Call* magazine. *On Call* is published by BostonWorks, a division of the *Boston Globe*.

Humor

Starting Points

Healthcare is admittedly serious business. While there are many conversations about life-and-death issues that cannot and should not be taken lightly, there also are occasions when a dose of humor can help build rapport, facilitate learning, and improve understanding. Indeed, humor is a powerful tool that providers can use to enhance communication and to demonstrate their compassion and humanity.

Humor has both emotional and physiologic benefits. For example, when people laugh they tend to feel better, think more clearly, and be more at ease and less stressed. Humor can also help bring about physiologic benefits such as increased respiration and oxygenation as well as bolstered immune systems. And when patients and providers share funny experiences or laugh together, they can develop rapport that helps them cope with frustrating or awkward situations.

A nurse was teaching a new mother how to take her baby's temperature. This mother spoke little English and was obviously nervous, scared, and in pain from her recent Cesarean section. While demonstrating how to shake a thermometer, the nurse accidentally hit it against the side of the crib. The new mother looked wide-eyed at the broken glass all over the floor but quickly broke into a smile when the nurse put on a clown nose she carries for occasions like these. The silly nose helped convey the nurse's feeling that "I feel like a clown when I do something like this." After a good laugh together, the nurse could again teach the new mother how to safely shake down—but not break—a thermometer. From Carol Schlef, RNC, MSW of SSM St. Mary's Health Center in St. Louis, Missouri.

Strategies, Ideas, and Suggestions

Types of humor. Humor includes jokes, riddles, word play, visual gags, and silly objects or cartoons. Consider the other person's learning style, age, culture, and gender when choosing which (if any) type of humor to use. One way to gauge the other person's sense of humor is by noting how he or she reacts to funny pictures in the room or silly pins you are wearing.

Timing. Humor should be used in small doses and not detract from treatment and care. Certainly there are times when humor is not appropriate, such as when people hear bad news. People may need to cry before they can laugh.

Bridge from humor to teaching. When teaching new concepts or treatment techniques, you might want to use humor in your introduction or as a way of keeping people interested and engaged. For example, you might heighten teenagers' interest in proper nutrition by first showing them a special "food pyramid for teens." When the teens see refined sugar, fat, caffeine, and salt listed as the four major food groups, they can laugh at how ridiculous this diet is and be more receptive to learning about healthy foods to eat.

When humor backfires. Despite good planning and sensitivity, sometimes humor backfires and is not appropriate or appreciated.

If your attempts at being funny fall flat, quickly apologize and let the other person know that you are not trying to be hurtful. In turn, when someone tells you a joke that you find offensive, don't overreact. You might say something like "that's a creative way of looking at things" and then quickly change the subject.

Showing humor. Some people are funnier than others. If you're not comfortable telling jokes or being silly, you can show humor in quieter ways. For example, in your waiting room you might have magazines with great cartoons. Or maybe put up posters and photographs that make people smile. And, if your dress code permits, you can also show your sense of humor by what you wear—such as colorful neckties, silly pins, or doodads on your stethoscope. But most important of all, relax. Almost always, you can add a dose of humor just by being you.

Humor is a powerful tool that providers can use to enhance communication and demonstrate their compassion and humanity.

Sources to Learn More

Association for Applied and Therapeutic Humor. Available at http://www.aath.org. Accessed January 22, 2004.

Baum N, Henkel G, 2000. "Medicine, marketing, and mirth: Having fun with your medical practice," *Marketing Your Clinical Practice*. Gaithersburg, MD: Aspen Publishers, Inc.

Bennett HJ, 2003. "Humor in medicine," *Southern Medical Journal*, 96(12):1257–1261.

Berk RA, 2003. *Humor as An Instructional Defibrillator: Evidence-based Techniques in Teaching and Assessment*. Sterling, VA: Stylus Publishing.

Osborne H, 2003. "In other words…adding a dose of humor to your patient teaching," *On Call* magazine, 6(7):16–17. Available at http://www.healthliteracy.com. Accessed January 22, 2004. Information is adapted and reprinted with permission of *On Call* magazine. *On Call* is published by BostonWorks, a division of the *Boston Globe*.

Robinson VM, 1991. *Humor and the Health Professions*. Thorofare, NJ: Slack, Inc.

Schlef C, 1999. *Mosby's Maternal–Newborn Patient Teaching Guides.* St. Louis, MO: Mosby, Inc.

Carol Schlef, RNC, MSW, is a women's health educator at SSM St. Mary's Health Center in St. Louis, Missouri. She is also the founder of a professional speaking business, Humor, Health, and Hugs. You can reach her by email at carol@humorhealthhugs.com or visit her website at http://www.humorhealthhugs.com. Accessed January 22, 2004.

World Laughter Tour. Available at http://www.worldlaughtertour.com. Accessed January 22, 2004.

Internet Information

Starting Points

Many people look to the Internet (websites) for health information. They not only go online after appointments but may search for information beforehand to help them decide whether a medical visit is really necessary. In fact, searching the Internet for health or medical information is one of the most popular online activities today. According to a recent survey, "fully 80% of adult Internet users, or about 93 million Americans, have searched for at least one of 16 major health topics online" (Fox and Fallows, 2003).

The benefits of the Internet are many. Regardless of their age, location, or disability, most people can go online provided they have basic computer capacity and a minimal amount of technical know-how. They can access information on almost every health topic, at times that are convenient, and communicate with others who share their concerns.

But the Internet also has drawbacks. People without access to home computers or high-speed connections may need to use shared computers at public facilities like libraries and senior centers. People may also find poorly-designed websites which are exceptionally difficult to navigate by those with limited physical, cognitive, literacy, or language skills. And, perhaps the biggest drawback of all, Internet users must determine for themselves the quality of online information.

Despite its drawbacks, the Internet as a tool of healthcare communication is here to stay. Used well and used wisely, the Internet supplements—not replaces—in-person clinical encounters. Before appointments, patients can prepare by learning a little about their medical condition or health concerns. During treatment, they may search for information about procedures, medications, clinical trials, and insurance benefits. And, on an ongoing basis, people may choose to participate in online chat rooms and support groups.

Debi's son has been diagnosed with a rare genetic disorder. Juggling two part-time jobs plus being the sole caretaker for her son, she seldom finds time to attend regional meetings of families living with this same disorder.

So Debi went online and found a virtual support group. Logging on in the evening after her son is in bed, Debi meets and "talks" with other parents who know firsthand the challenges she and her son are facing. Debi finds this group invaluable and says that it gives her the information and encouragement she needs to advocate for her son each day.

Strategies, Ideas, and Suggestions

When patients bring you Internet information. Patients today may bring you folders full of Internet information. Sometimes, you may be familiar with the information they bring. Other times the information may be new to you. And you may or may not find this Internet information credible, accurate, or relevant.

Regardless of your opinion about its quality, thank patients for their Internet research. Agree to read their print-outs and get back to them with feedback. If you disagree with the Internet information, however, don't be surprised when patients are disappointed. Studies show that patients often overrate the value of Internet information and assume that, just because it is on the Internet, it is correct (Peterson and Fretz, 2003).

Teach patients how to search the Internet. People tend to search for health information only on an as-needed basis, when they (or a family member or friend) are newly diagnosed or given a new medication. Since they are not regular visitors to any one site, it is particularly important that people know how to evaluate the quality of information they find.

You can help by suggesting people look at:

- The organization that hosts the site. Is it unbiased or advertising a product?
- The credentials of the writer(s), contributor(s), and those on the editorial board. Are they credible experts or just giving opinions?
- Contact information. Does the site include a mailing address as well as phone number?
- The date that the site was last reviewed or updated. Has the site been reviewed within the past year?

Internet Information

Online support groups. Online support groups can be important sources of information and emotional support. Benefits include the fact that people can exchange strategies and just-in-time encouragement with those in similar situations. This can be particularly important for people with rare diseases. As well, the Internet is convenient and people can participate at any time and don't usually have to leave their homes to do so. Also, some people like online groups because they can participate anonymously.

On the downside, online groups lack face-to-face interaction. Participants may not trust (perhaps, appropriately so) those they never meet in person. Also, conversations may at times go beyond simply sharing information and include misinformation or verge on gossip.

Recommended websites. To help patients find accurate, readable, up-to-date, and unbiased Internet information, provide lists of sites you feel are credible. Make sure to include a disclaimer, however, noting that you cannot guarantee the accuracy of information people find.

Here are a few well-regarded sites:

- American Academy of Family Physicians, http://www.familydoctor.org
- Centers for Disease Control and Prevention (English, Spanish, and other languages), http://www.cdc.gov
- MEDLINEplus, from the U.S. National Library of Medicine (English and Spanish), http://www.nlm.nih.gov/medlineplus
- Mercksource.com, http://mercksource.com
- National Cancer Institute, http://www.cancer.gov
- National Institutes of Health, http://www.nih.gov
- NOAH: New York Online Access to Health (English and Spanish), http://www.noah-health.org

Used well and used wisely, the Internet supplements—not replaces—in-person clinical encounters.

Sources to Learn More

Fox S, Fallows D, 2003. *Internet Health Resources, Pew Internet & American Life Project.* Available at http://www.pewinternet.org. Accessed January 28, 2004.

Internet is valued for health information seekers, *Drug Benefit Trends*, 15(8):8–11, 2003. Available at http://www.medscape.com/viewarticle/461426_print. Accessed January 23, 2004.

Internet report: Surveying the digital future year three, 2003. Los Angeles, University of California. Available at http://ccp.ucla.edu/pdf/UCLA-Internet-Report-Year-Three.pdf. Accessed January 23, 2004.

Lewis D, 2003. "Computers in patient education," *Computers, Informatics, Nursing*, 21(2):88–96.

Masys DR, 2002. "Effects of current and future information technologies on the health care workforce," *Health Affairs*, 21(5):33–41.

Peterson MW, Fretz PC, 2003. "Patient use of the Internet for information in a lung cancer clinic," *CHEST*, 123(2):452–457.

Schloman BF, 2002. "Quality of health information on the web: Where are we now?," *Online Journal of Issues in Nursing*, December 16.

Tate DF, Jackvony EH, Wing RR, 2003. "Effects of Internet behavioral counseling on weight loss in adults at risk for type 2 diabetes," *JAMA*, 289(14):1833–1836

Computer and Internet Use, U.S. Department of Commerce/ National TeleCommunications and Information Association. Available at http://www.ntia.doc.gov/ntiahome/dn/html/Chapter2.htm. Accessed January 23, 2004.

Weinert C, 2000. "Social support in cyberspace for women with chronic illness," *Rehabilitation Nursing*, 25(4):129–135.

Wofford JL, Currin D, Michielutte R, Wofford MM, 2001. "The multimedia computer for low-literacy patient education: A pilot project of cancer risk perceptions," *Medscape General Medicine*, 3(2).

Internet Information

Interpreters: Foreign and American Sign Language

Starting Points

Today, patients, families, and caregivers must be knowledgeable about their treatment and care responsibilities. While this is always a challenge, it is even more difficult when patients and providers do not share a common language. As more than 46 million people in the United States today speak a language other than English at home, this language gap often occurs (U.S. Census, 2004).

Interpreters can help. They take the words one person says and convert them into the language another person understands. This can be with foreign languages such as English to Hindi, or with American Sign Language (ASL) used by many people in the Deaf community.

Professional medical interpreters are the best source of help. They not only are trained in medical vocabulary but are also instructed in how to maintain neutrality and not impose their personal views. As well, trained interpreters will look up unfamiliar terms to make sure they interpret them correctly. When onsite trained medical interpreters are not available, organizations often turn to over-the-phone interpretation services like Language Line (http://www.languageline.com).

Another option, though not a recommended one, is to use bilingual family or volunteers. The problem with these untrained interpreters is that, despite their best intentions, they sometimes make errors, misjudgments, and misstatements. Violations of privacy and confidentiality are also concerns. Children, especially, should not interpret for their parents or other family members. Doing so can place them in the midst of health conversations they shouldn't be a part of.

Professional interpreter services are not optional in some health organizations. States, such as the Commonwealth of Massachusetts, require that acute-care hospitals provide interpreter services in connection with all emergency care for non-English speaking patients (Commonwealth of Massachusetts, 2000). In addition to being required by law, interpreter services can also improve patient care.

"Lydia," an elderly Russian-speaking woman, was in the hospital recovering from surgery. Late one evening, Lydia was making motions on her chest. The night nurse wasn't sure if Lydia was having chest pain or was trying to tell her something, so she paged the medical interpreter to clarify. Over the phone, the interpreter asked the patient if she was having chest pain. Lydia responded, "My heart hurts because my daughter hasn't come to visit me, and I'm feeling sad." Once she had that piece of information, the nurse was able to appropriately intervene and help Lydia deal with her sadness.

Strategies, Ideas, and Suggestions

Welcome patients. Help patients feel welcome, even when you do not share a common language or way of communicating. You might, for example, sign "hello" or greet patients in their native tongue. Even if you mangle pronunciation, it is still evident that at least you cared enough to try.

Working with interpreters. Allow sufficient time when using interpreters as conversations may take two to three times longer than usual. Ideally, arrange your schedule to talk briefly with interpreters before and after patient meetings. Look and speak directly with the patient, not the interpreter. You not only show respect this way but also can notice a patient's non-verbal cues.

When working with an ASL interpreter, the interpreter should sit a little behind and to the side of the health provider. This way, the patient can see both the provider and interpreter in the same visual field. The provider, in turn, can listen to the interpreter while looking directly at the patient.

When interpreters are not available. There invariably will be times when you need to communicate with non-English speaking patients and a qualified interpreter is not available. In these instances, translated tools of basic phrases can help though they admittedly are not as good as working with an interpreter. Tools like these are especially helpful when asking basic questions like "Are you hungry?" or "Are you in pain?" as they have several response choices including "Yes," "No," and "I don't know." To use these tools, however, patients must be able to read in their native languages and the phrases must be accurately translated. *Pocket Medical Spanish* is an example of a translated tool. (To learn more, go to http://www.booksmythe.com).

You might also communicate basic health messages with visuals, pictographs, and objects or models. For example, you might draw a pictograph (simple line drawing) of a side effect like pain or nausea. Or encourage patients to show you on an anatomic model how they will check for infection. As well, visual pain scales can help non-English speaking patients express the intensity of their discomfort—allowing them to point to a facial expression of how much pain they are in. The FACES Pain Rating Scale is an example, and is available at http://www3.us.elsevierhealth.com/WOW/faces.html.

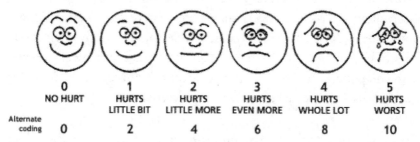

Figure 1.1. FACES Pain Rating Scale. Source: From Wong D. L., Hochenberry-Eaton M., Wilson D., Winkelstein M. L., Schwartz P. Wongs Essentials of Pediatric Nursing, ed. 6, St. Louis, 2001, p. 1301. Copyrighted by Mosby, Inc. Reprinted by permission.

Culture. Even when patients hear familiar words or see them signed by an interpreter, they may not grasp the concepts you are talking about. Understanding the disease process is an example. In the United States, it is commonly accepted that germs and viruses cause disease. But people from other cultural perspectives may be equally certain that diseases are caused by an imbalance of mind and body. With conceptual differences like these, it is no wonder that those from other languages and lands may have difficulty comprehending how medical interventions like surgery and medication can help.

Culture also means learning—not assuming—how much patients want to know about their medical conditions, who should be involved in decision-making, and to what extent patients are familiar with physiology and medical procedures. Often, trained interpreters can help bridge cultural differences like these. (To learn about language and culture, go to Language and Culture: Communicating with People from Other Languages and Lands on page 123.)

Body language. Beyond words, some gestures and body language are not universally understood. While feelings of anger and happiness may look alike around the world, even "yes" and "no" are sometimes communicated in different ways. In the United States for example, it is assumed that a nod means "yes" while in other languages, a nod may simply mean "I hear what you said."

Notice signs of difficulty. Regardless of language differences, it is the health provider's responsibility to make sure that medical information is communicated accurately. If you sense that there is a problem, such as lengthy conversations between the interpreter and patient and only one-word answers to you, check with another interpreter to make sure the message is being communicated correctly.

Technology. Until recently, interpreters always needed to be in the same room as patients and providers. Today, video relay services and other advanced technology make it possible for interpreters, patients, and clinicians to communicate from three separate locations. Be aware, however, that there is the potential for error and inconvenience when equipment fails to work well, or at all. Also, in all off-site situations, be particularly sensitive to issues of patient confidentiality.

Verify understanding. Just as when communicating in English, ask patients to tell you, via interpreters, how they understand information "no" answers. Instead, ask open-ended questions like, "How would you take this medicine?" rather than "Do you understand what to do?"

Look and speak directly with the patient, not the interpreter. You not only show respect this way but also can notice a patient's non-verbal cues.

Sources to Learn More

An Act Requiring Competent Interpreter Services in the Delivery of Certain Acute Health Care Services. The Commonwealth of Massachusetts. Chapter 66, H 4917. Signed into law by Governor Cellucci on April 14, 2000.

American Translator Association. Available online at http://www.atanet.org. Accessed January 23, 2004.

Andrulis D, Goodman N, Pryor C, 2002. "What a difference an interpreter can make: Health care experiences of uninsured with limited English proficiency," *The Access Project,* Boston, MA.

Buchwald D, et al, 1993. "The medical interview across cultures," *Patient Care,* April 15:152–162.

Cross Cultural Health Care Program. Available at http://www.xculture.org. Accessed January 23, 2004.

Dollinger RK, 1992. *Pocket Medical Spanish.* Van Nuys, CA: Booksmythe. Available at http://www.booksmythe.com. Accessed January 18, 2004.

FACES Pain Rating Scale, Wong on the Web. Available at http://www3.us.elsevierhealth.com/WOW/faces.html. Accessed January 28, 2004.

Flores G, Laws MB, Mayo SJ, et al, 2003. "Errors in medical interpretation and their potential clinical consequences in pediatric encounters," *Pediatrics,* 111(1):6–14.

Language Line Services. Available at http://www.languageline.com. Accessed January 23, 2004.

Lipson JG, Dibble SL, Minarik PA, (ed.), 1996. *Culture and Nursing Care: A Pocket Guide.* San Francisco, CA:UCSF Nursing Press.

Osborne H, 2003a. "In other words...communicating about health with new immigrants," *On Call* magazine, 6(10):16–17. Available at http://www.healthliteracy.com. Accessed January 23, 2004. Information is adapted and reprinted with permission of *On Call* magazine. *On Call* is published by BostonWorks, a division of the *Boston Globe.*

———, 2003b. "In other words...communicating about health with ASL," *On Call* magazine, 6(6):16–17. Available at http://www.healthliteracy.com. Accessed January 22, 2004. Information is adapted and reprinted with permission of *On Call* magazine. *On Call* is published by BostonWorks, a division of the *Boston Globe.*

_____, 2000a. *Overcoming Communication Barriers in Patient Education.* Gaithersburg, MD: Aspen Publishers, Inc. Information is adapted and reprinted with the author's permission.

_____, 2000b. "In other words...when you truly need to find other words...working with medical interpreters," *On Call* magazine, 3(7):38–39. Available at http://www.healthliteracy.com. Accessed January 23, 2004. Information is adapted and reprinted with permission of *On Call* magazine. *On Call* is published by BostonWorks, a division of the *Boston Globe.*

Putsch RW, 1985. "Cross-cultural communication: The special case of interpreters in health care," *JAMA*, 254(23):170–174.

U.S. Census. Available online at http://factfinder.census.gov. Accessed January 23, 2004.

Interpreters

Knowledge: Learning and Teaching

Starting Points

All patient-provider encounters are opportunities to learn, teach, and exchange knowledge. Ideally, these encounters include mutual learning in which providers educate patients about their diagnosis and treatment options and patients enlighten providers about their symptoms, values, and willingness to participate in treatment and care.

People of all ages want to know what new diagnoses or treatments will mean in their lives and how to cope with their medical conditions on a day-to-day basis. How this should be taught, however, may vary depending on a person's learning style. Some people are auditory learners and learn best when listening to lectures or reading instructions aloud. Others are visual learners who understand by looking at pictures or charts. And still others are kinesthetic learners who absorb information when touching objects or doing activities. Often, people have more than one learning style and learn best through a combination of these activities.

Age also affects how people learn. School-aged children, for example, might relate to topics best when they hear about famous people who have the same diagnosis. And they might master self-care concepts by first practicing them on computer games. Older adults, though, may benefit from teaching that takes into account any physical, sensory, or cognitive changes. For example, when someone has trouble concentrating you might teach just small amounts of new information in each session.

Adult learning theory, as outlined by Malcolm Knowles (Knowles, 1990), is an excellent framework to use when educating most adults. Teaching starts with each learner's questions and concerns and then focuses on practical information to address them. Throughout the educational process, teachers and learners (or providers and patients) collaborate to ensure understanding. Principles of adult learning theory include:

- *Adults are motivated to learn as they experience needs and interests that learning will satisfy.* This means, focus on topics that are of immediate concern to the learner.

- *Adults' orientation to learning is life-centered.* Teach practical information that the learner can apply in his or her daily life.

- *Experience is the richest resource for adults' learning.* Compare and contrast new information with what the learner already is familiar with and understands.

- *Adults have a deep need to be self-directing.* Encourage learners to help set the educational agenda—what needs to be taught now and what can wait until the next session. (Adapted from Knowles, 1990 and Osborne, 2002)

Forty-seven-year-old Wilma just learned that she has diabetes. In the first appointment after her diagnosis, the health provider plans to teach about diabetes physiology as well as basic medication, nutrition, and exercise information. But Wilma appears uninterested and distracted. When asked, Wilma talks about her great-aunt who died of diabetes when she was only fifty-one years old.

Appreciating Wilma's immediate concern, her provider talks instead about the fact that, once her diabetes is well-controlled, Wilma is at low risk for dying from this disease. Once her fears and concerns are addressed, Wilma is ready and motivated to learn about the specific ways she can now manage her diabetes.

Strategies, Ideas, and Suggestions

Create an environment that supports learning. Healthcare settings can be difficult environments in which to teach and learn. There are often distractions, noises, and interruptions. Privacy can be hard to find. Whenever possible, minimize these disruptions and create environments more conducive to learning. This can mean finding quiet spaces in which to meet, or closing curtains and sitting across from each other to create a sense of privacy. A good learning environment also has few visual distractions. Minimize the number of signs and posters on your walls as well as clutter on your desk. Make sure, too, that you do not appear stressed or pressed for time. Your tension is likely to be noticed and can have a negative impact on learning.

Teach when patients are ready to learn. Timing is often as important as content, for patients may be unable to learn when they are distracted or uncomfortable. Take your cues from patients about how much information to present in each session. For example, if a person seems to "tune out" after a short while, consider scheduling a follow-up meeting instead of one long session. Make sure to also teach when people are interested and can apply what they learn. If a person is anticipating surgery, for example, he or she may be more receptive to information about anesthesia rather than rehabilitation.

Teach relevant content. Adults want to learn information that relates to their immediate interests, concerns, and fears. For example, Robert and Philip are both diagnosed with colon cancer. Robert may want to know about genetic links as he is worried about his children's risk. Philip, instead, might be more concerned about how chemotherapy will affect his ability to work.

Do not overload patients with more information than they want and are able to handle, for it can make people feel stressed and confused. People will almost always ask for more information when they are interested and ready to learn.

Start with what is known and proceed to the unknown. Build on familiar information, tying new learning to old. For example, instead of talking in general about proper body mechanics you might instead teach a new mother how to properly pick up her baby. Make sure, as well, to find out what patients already know or believe to be true. Sometimes you need to clarify misconceptions and correct misunderstandings before introducing new information.

Pace. Not everyone learns at the same rate. Watch for cues that you are going either too fast or too slow by observing whether people look "glazed over" or their body language indicates they are bored. You can also ask people if you are teaching at a good pace. This is admittedly easier to do when meeting one-to-one. But, even when teaching a group, you can check the pace by stopping periodically and giving people the opportunity to ask questions and practice or demonstrate what they are learning.

Repetition. Give a "heads up" about the topics you plan to discuss. Talk about topics one at a time, and make sure that patients understand each key point before moving to the next. At the end of teaching sessions, summarize main ideas and topics. Be consistent; use the same terminology and demonstrate techniques the same way each time.

Use a variety of teaching methods. To meet the needs of people who are auditory, visual, and kinesthetic learners, make sure to use a variety of teaching strategies. For instance, when teaching Michelle about asthma, you might talk with her about the condition (auditory), show her a model of a lung and let her try using an inhaler (kinesthetic), and give her flash cards to look at or booklets to read when she is at home (visual).

Encourage patients to be active learners. People learn best when they are actively involved in the learning process and not just passive recipients of information. Ask patients what they want to learn and, together, set the teaching agenda. Make sure that you allow plenty of opportunities for interaction, with sufficient time for patients to ask questions and raise concerns. And, of course, provide lists of resources for people who want to learn more.

Confirm understanding. The goal of all learning and teaching is knowledge. Make sure that people truly understand and can use the information you are presenting. Stop periodically and make sure that patients are keeping up with you. You can do this by asking people to tell you, in their own words, what they understand you to say or show you how they will accomplish skills you just taught. As knowledge is a two-way process, make sure to also confirm that you understand what patients are teaching you.

Talk about the topics one at a time, and make sure that patients understand each key point before moving to the next.

Sources to Learn More

Bastable S, 1997. *Nurse as Educator: Principles of Learning and Teaching.* Sudbury, MA: Jones and Bartlett Publishers.

Breckon D, et al, 1998. *Community Health Education: Settings, Roles, and Skills for the 21st Century,* 4th ed. Gaithersburg, MD: Aspen Publishers, Inc.

Falvo DR, 2004. *Effective Patient Education: A Guide to Increased Compliance.* Sudbury, MA: Jones and Bartlett Publishers.

Farwell T, (date unavailable). "Visual, auditory, kinesthetic: Which is your child?," *Family Education Network.* Available at http://familyeducation.com/article/0, 1120,3-605,00.html. Accessed January 28, 2004.

Hayes KS, 1998. "Randomized trial of geragogy-based medication instruction in the emergency department," *Nursing Research,* 47(4):211–218.

Knowles M, 1990. *The Adult Learner: A Neglected Species,* 4th ed. Houston, TX: Gulf Publishing Company.

_____, 1980. *The Modern Practice of Adult Education: From Pedagogy to Andragogy.* Englewood Cliffs, NJ: Cambridge Adult Education.

Osborne H, 2002. *Partnering with Patients To Improve Health Outcomes.* Gaithersburg, MD: Aspen Publishers, Inc. Information is adapted and reprinted with the author's permission.

_____, 2001a. "In other words…mind what you say…speaking with and listening to older adults," *On Call* magazine, 4(6):50–52. Available at http://www.healthliteracy.com. Accessed January 18, 2004. Information is adapted and reprinted with permission of *On Call* magazine. *On Call* is published by BostonWorks, a division of the *Boston Globe.*

_____, 2001b. "In other words…start where they are…communicating with children and their families about health and illness," *On Call* magazine, 4(3):46–47. Available at http://www.healthliteracy.com. Accessed January 23, 2004. Information is adapted and reprinted with permission of *On Call* magazine. *On Call* is published by BostonWorks, a division of the *Boston Globe.*

_____, 2000. "In other words…making sure it works…documenting patient education," *On Call* magazine, 3(2):38–39. Available at http://www.healthliteracy.com. Accessed January 23, 2004.

Pearson M, Wessman J, 1996. Gerogogy, *Home Healthcare Nurse,* 14(8):631–636.

Redman BK, 1993. *The Process of Patient Education,* 7th ed. St. Louis, MO: Mosby-Year Book.

———, 1997. *The Practice of Patient Education,* 8th ed. St. Louis, MO: Mosby-Year Book, Inc.

Language and Culture: Communicating with People from Other Languages and Lands

Starting Points

Accessing, using, and understanding the United States healthcare system is difficult for almost everyone. But for people who speak limited English or come from other cultures and lands, these tasks can seem impossible. For example, people may not know which health services or resources they can use, or they may not understand the medical instructions their providers are talking about or giving them to read. As the United States becomes increasingly diverse, situations like these are becoming more common.

In terms of language, it generally takes people from two years to a life time to become fluent. With limited English, people may have sufficient social language to talk about the food or weather. But, until they are truly fluent, people are unlikely to have the language skills they need to discuss "how" and "why"—the type of information common in health communication.

Culture, too, impacts how people understand and make sense of health information. People bring their individual experiences, values, customs, and logic to each new situation. For example, those from parts of the world where resources are scarce may not be familiar with health screening and early detection activities. Therefore, they may not understand why mammograms, pap smears, and blood pressure checks are recommended.

Even people from the same country may be of different cultures. In the United States for example, there are regional and local differences. For example, a person from the south may want grits for breakfast while someone living in the north prefers oatmeal. These cultural differences extend beyond food choices and can indeed affect how people understand and act on health information.

Despite cultural and linguistic differences, health providers must communicate in ways all of their patients can understand. This is more than just good patient care. It is also the law. Under title IV of the U.S. Civil Rights Act of 1964, health professionals are responsible for bridging communication gaps with patients who speak other languages and come from other lands.

Communication experts have yet to agree whether it is best to create separate messages for every cultural group or, instead, have a single communication that appeals to a more varied population. Industries such as advertising and toy manufacturing seem to be taking a somewhat flexible approach. For example, one toy company has created a doll that looks ethnically ambiguous—with tawny skin, dark hair, and facial features that are common to several ethnic groups. It seems the manufacturer expects that children from many cultural backgrounds will be able to relate to this doll.

Health organizations might adopt this approach. When organizations lack the resources to meet all of their patients' cultural and linguistic needs, perhaps they might focus their efforts on creating one message that most patients can relate to and understand. This solution, of course, is dependent on each organization's policies, practices, and guidelines.

Strategies, Ideas, and Suggestions

Create a welcoming atmosphere. Welcome patients by displaying multicultural artifacts, globes, and worldwide maps. Translated signs are important, as well. Greet patients in their native languages and ask how to pronounce their names correctly. Even if your pronunciation is less than perfect, you have conveyed a willingness to communicate despite linguistic differences. Encourage your office staff to also set a welcoming tone. They can do this by asking patients if they need interpreters or want help filling out health histories and other written forms.

Interpreters. Interpreters work with the spoken word, communicating what one person says in words and terms another person understands. When talking about important health information with patients who speak limited or no English, try to work with

Language and Culture

trained medical interpreters rather than bilingual family, friends, or volunteers. Trained interpreters are educated not only in medical vocabulary, ethics, and confidentiality but also can act as "cultural brokers" to present information in keeping with a person's cultural beliefs and practices. (For more information on interpreters, go to Interpreters: Foreign and American Sign Languages on page 109.)

Translations. Translators work with the written word, taking information from one language to another. Beyond words, translated materials should be culturally appropriate and include graphics and examples that readers can accept and relate to. Generally, it takes a team to do this well. At a minimum, this team should include the translator, clinicians, and those who understand the culture of the intended audience. (To learn more, go to Translations on page 231.)

Translating information is a multi-step process. Allow sufficient time to:

- translate materials from English to the new language.
- "back translate" information from the new language back to English.
- design and layout materials in ways that enhance understanding.
- field test the translated material with intended readers.
- make necessary revisions and test again to make sure you didn't add new problems.

Talking. When talking with people who speak limited English, focus on essential, need-to-know skills and behaviors rather than nice-to-know background information. Speak at a slower pace, pausing for two or three seconds after asking questions or giving new information. But do not speak louder just because people have limited English—this can come across as sounding angry and does nothing to improve communication.

Whenever possible, use common words like "cancer" rather than "oncology," or "kidney doctor" and not "nephrologist." Avoid medical jargon and acronyms like "BP" when you can just as simply say "blood pressure." Be aware that some words are easier to explain than others. In Vietnamese, for example, there is no term that translates for "cervix," and it takes many words to explain what a cervix is, where it is located, and how it functions in the body.

Body language. Whether you communicate through an interpreter or talk directly with patients, pay as much attention to nonverbal communication as you do to words. Notice the volume and speed at which people speak and pay attention to their silences, as well. Look also at posture, gestures, and eye contact. Be cautious, however, about making assumptions because in some cultures it is considered rude to look other people in the eye. Be aware of your own nonverbal communication as well and make sure you are interacting in ways that are welcoming and respectful.

Other ways of communicating. Instead of, or in addition to, working with interpreters and translators, find additional ways to communicate your health message. This includes pictographs (simple line drawings that show ideas or actions), diagrams, demonstrations, stories, and gestures. Be sensitive, however, to the fact that gestures can have more than one meaning and are sometimes misunderstood. Consider "hands-on" practice, as well. For example, instead of just telling patients how to take a new liquid medication, use an actual dosing spoon to demonstrate and then have the patient re-demonstrate how to measure and take the medication.

Patients' perspectives. Rather than assume, ask patients about their perspective of illness and treatment. You can fashion your questions along the lines of those from Dr. Arthur Kleinman:

- What do you think is wrong?
- What caused it?

- What do you want me to do?

- What is the chief way this illness (or treatment) has affected your life?

- What do you fear most about this illness (or treatment)? (Kleinman, 1989)

Decision-maker. In some cultures, patients are not the ones to make health decisions. Find out whether the patient, entire family, or a specifically designated decision-maker accepts this responsibility. Make sure to include this person when discussing diagnostic information and making treatment decisions.

Confirm understanding. When communicating with patients from other languages and lands, do not assume that a nod and a smile means your message is understood. To confirm that patients understand, ask an open-ended question such as, "How will you...?" rather than a yes/no question like, "Do you know how to...?" When it appears that the other person does not understand, find other ways to communicate the same message.

Communication experts have yet to agree whether it is best to create separate messages for every cultural group or, instead, have a single communication that appeals to a more varied population.

Sources to Learn More

Doak CC, Doak LG, Root JH, 1996. *Teaching Patients with Low Literacy Skills,* 2nd ed. Philadelphia, PA: J.B. Lippincott Company.

Dollinger RK, 1992. *Pocket Medical Spanish.* Van Nuys, CA: Booksmythe. Available at http://www.booksmythe.com. Accessed January 18, 2004.

Ensuring Linguistic Access in Health Care Settings: An Overview of Current Legal Rights and Responsibilities. Kaiser Commission on the Medicaid and the Uninsured. Available at http://www.kff.org/uninsured/kcmu4131report.cfm. Accessed January 24, 2004.

Fadiman A, 1997. *The Spirit Catches You and You Fall Down: A Hmong Child, Her American Doctors & The Collision of Two Cultures.* New York: Noonday Press.

Institute of Medicine, 2002. *Speaking of Health*. Washington, D.C.: The
National Academies Press.

Kleinman A, 1989. *The Illness Narratives: Suffering, Healing and the Human Condition*. New York, NY: Basic Books.

Lipson JG, Dibble SL, and Minarik PA, eds., 1996. *Culture and Nursing Care: A Pocket Guide*. San Francisco, CA: UCSF Nursing Press.

McKinney J, Kurtz-Rossi S, 2000. *Culture, Health, and Literacy: A Guide to Health Education Materials for Adults with Limited English Literacy Skills*.
Boston, MA: World Education. Available at http://www.worlded.org/publications.html. Accessed January 24, 2004.

McGee J, 1999. *Writing and Designing Print Materials for Beneficiaries: A Guide for State Medicaid Agencies*. HCFA Publication Number 10145. Baltimore,
MD: Centers for Medicare & Medicaid Services, U.S. Department of Health
and Human Services. (A second edition is forthcoming in 2004. For ordering
information, contact Jeanne McGee, McGee & Evers Consulting, Inc., Vancouver, Washington, 360-574-4744, jmcgee@pacifier.com).

National Institute for Literacy/LINCS. A large database of adult education and
literacy resources in the United States including LINCSearch, MyLINCS, the
Health & Literacy Special Collection/Compendium, and NIFL-Health (an
online discussion group about health and literacy). Available at
http://www.nifl.gov/lincs. Accessed January 24, 2004.

Osborne H, 2003. "In other words...communicating about health with new
immigrants," *On Call* magazine, 6(10):16–17. Available at http://www.health-literacy.com. Accessed January 23, 2004. Information is adapted and reprinted
with permission of *On Call* magazine. *On Call* is published by BostonWorks, a
division of the *Boston Globe*.

_____, 2002. *Partnering with Patients To Improve Health Outcomes*. Gaithersburg, MD: Aspen Publishers, Inc. Information is adapted and reprinted with
the author's permission.

_____, 2000a. *Overcoming Communication Barriers in Patient Education*.
Gaithersburg, MD: Aspen Publishers, Inc. Information is adapted and
reprinted with the author's permission.

_____, 2000b. "In other words...when you truly need to find other
words...working with medical interpreters," *On Call* magazine, 3(7):38–39.
Available at http://www.healthliteracy.com. Accessed January 23, 2004. Information is adapted and reprinted with permission of *On Call* magazine. *On
Call* is published by BostonWorks, a division of the *Boston Globe*.

_____, 2000c. "In other words...it takes more than just words...culturally and
linguistically appropriate materials," *On Call* magazine, 3(4):34–35. Available
at http://www.healthliteracy.com. Accessed January 23, 2004. Information is

Language and Culture

adapted and reprinted with permission of *On Call* magazine. *On Call* is published by BostonWorks, a division of the *Boston Globe*.

_____, 1999. "In other words... communicating with people from other cultures," *On Call* magazine, 2(8):42–43. Available at http://ww.healthliteracy.com. Accessed January 23, 2004. Information is adapted and reprinted with permission of *On Call* magazine. *On Call* is published by BostonWorks, a division of the *Boston Globe*.

Singleton K, 2002. "Health literacy and adult English language learners," *ERIC Q&A*. Available at http://www.cal.org/ncle/digests/healthlitQA.htm. Accessed January 24, 2004.

United States Census 2000, "Language use and English-speaking ability: 2000," U.S. Department of Commerce, Economics and Statistics Administration. Available at http://factfinder.census.gov. Accessed January 24, 2004.

Walker R, 2003. "Whassup, Barbie?," *Boston Sunday Globe*, January 12, 2003.

Literacy: Communicating with People Who Do Not Read or Read Well

Starting Points

People who struggle with literacy almost always have trouble understanding health information because so much of it is communicated in writing. For example, people with limited literacy may take medication incorrectly because they cannot read prescription labels. Or they might not prepare properly for outpatient procedures because they do not interpret instruction sheets correctly.

These reading tasks require functional literacy skills—defined as "the ability to use printed and written information to function in society, to achieve one's goals, and to develop one's knowledge and potential" (Kirsch, et al., 1993). Literacy includes a subset of three skills:

- *Prose literacy*—needed to understand and use text found in materials like newspapers, magazines, and books
- *Document literacy*—required for items such as applications, schedules, forms, maps, graphs, and tables
- *Quantitative literacy*—necessary for arithmetic operations such as those found on bank forms and purchase orders (Kirsch, et al., 1993)

But many people lack these literacy skills. A nationwide study by the United States National Adult Literacy Survey (NALS) in 1992 (the most recent data available) found that nearly half of all adults in the United States have, at most, only marginal literacy skills. This means they are apt to have trouble understanding complex text, filling out bank statements, and using maps or schedules. The International Adult Literacy Survey (IALS) looked at people's literacy level in 23 countries and found similar results.

People have trouble reading for many reasons. Researchers have found that people's literacy levels are often tied to their socio-economic background, level of education, and workforce experience. Also, reading difficulties may be due to strokes, dementia, stress, medication side effects, or learning and cognitive processing problems such as dyslexia. Regardless of the reasons why, when people struggle with reading their health can be in jeopardy.

Jim is of average intelligence but has dyslexia and can barely read. He went to the doctor for a chronic cough and was told he needed an X-ray. Jim went to a medical center where he hadn't been before and looked for signs saying "X-ray." He didn't see any and was unaware that he needed to instead follow the signs to the "Radiology Department."

The closest word Jim saw to "X-ray" was "Exit." Frustrated and unwilling to let others know that he can barely read, Jim left the medical center and didn't return. Unfortunately, his cough went undiagnosed and untreated.

—A true story told by an adult learner

Strategies, Ideas, and Suggestions

Know about reading difficulties. For many, illiteracy is a great source of shame. It seldom is advisable to ask people directly if they can read. Instead, set a tone that is open and feels safe so people are more comfortable revealing any reading difficulties.

There is active discussion within the health literacy community about whether routine literacy testing makes sense in clinical situations. Many think that even well-regarded tests like the REALM (Rapid Estimate of Adult Literacy in Medicine) and TOFHLA (Test of Functional Health Literacy in Adults) are better for research, not the clinic.

Instead of formal tests like these, providers may choose to learn about their patient's learning styles and literacy skills by asking open-ended questions. For example, "Do you like to learn by watching TV, listening to the radio, talking with people, or reading?" Indeed, patients with limited literacy skills are apt to select non-reading options.

You can also get a sense of patients' literacy levels by noticing "red flags" of reading difficulties. For example, patients with limited reading skills may:

- "Forget" their eyeglasses or complain of headaches each time they are asked to complete paperwork.

- Identify medications by color and shape, not prescription label.

- Have a lot of misspelled words when they fill out forms.

- Always bring other people to help with reading tasks.

- Ask a lot of questions about topics already covered in hand-outs.

- Answer "no" to all health history questions so as to not get any follow-up questions.

- One way you <u>cannot</u> tell who has trouble with reading is by appearance. Poor readers dress, act, talk, and look just like everyone else, as stated in the American Medical Association video, "Low Health Literacy: You Can't Tell by Looking."

Logical order. Make it easy for people with limited reading skills (as well as most everyone else) to follow what you are saying by presenting health information in logical order. This means teaching one step at a time and letting people know what's next. For example, begin with "I am going to teach you how to check for an infection. Here are three things to know. First, you should ... second, you need to ... and third you must..." Reinforce these key points before introducing new ones. At the end, review all tasks that patients need to do.

Words. To help people better understand you and your colleagues along the continuum, use consistent words and terms. For example, agree whether to say "stitch" or "suture" when talking about closing wounds. If possible, use common one- and two-syllable words. But when more complicated words are truly needed, like "chemotherapy" or "bronchodilator," use them and give easy-to-understand examples.

When you must use medical jargon or acronyms like "HIPAA" or "GERD," make sure patients know what these terms mean. Try not to use words that sound alike such as "gait/gate," or have more than one meaning like "stool" and "dressing." (To learn more about words, go to Word Choice on page 257.)

Written materials. People with limited literacy skills may do best with easy-to-read materials written at a third- to fifth-grade reading level. In truth, there is not an abundance of health materials at this level. You don't need to avoid all written materials just because they are more difficult. Even those who struggle with reading may better comprehend when they are at home, relaxed, and have sufficient time. Also, patients may share written materials with others who can help explain information they do not understand.

Non-written alternatives. In addition to written materials, communicate health information in non-written ways such as with pictographs, objects, and videotapes. This way, patients have several formats to help them learn, understand, and remember.

Assess understanding. Make sure patients understand the information you are communicating. You can do this by asking them to tell you, in their own words, what you just discussed. A way that does NOT work well is to ask patients, "Do you understand?" Readers and nonreaders alike often respond by simply nodding "yes." When you find there is misunderstanding, rephrase (not just restate) whatever is not clear.

People who struggle with literacy almost always have trouble understanding health information because so much is communicated in writing.

Sources to Learn More

AMC Cancer Research Center, 1994. *Beyond the Brochure: Alternative Approaches to Effective Health Communication.* Center for Disease Control and Prevention. Available at http://www.cdc.gov/cancer/nbccedp. Accessed January 24, 2004.

American Medical Association, 2000. Low Health Literacy: You Can't Tell by Looking (video), as part of the *Health Literacy Introductory Kit*. Chicago, IL: American Medical Association and AMA Foundation.

Brandes WL, ed., 1996. *Literacy, Health, and the Law: An Exploration of the Law and the Plight of Marginal Reader Within the Healthcare System*. Philadelphia, PA: Health Promotion Council of Southeastern Pennsylvania, Inc.

Brown H, Prisuta R, Jacobs B, Campbell A, 1996. *Literacy of Older Adults in America*. National Center for Education Statistics. Washington, D.C.: U.S. Department of Education.

Doak CC, Doak LG, Root JH, 1996. *Teaching Patients with Low Literacy Skills*, 2nd ed. Philadelphia, PA: J.B. Lippincott Company.

Harvard School of Public Health, Health Literacy Studies, National Center for the Study of Adult Learning and Literacy. Available at http://www.hsph.harvard.edu/healthliteracy/links.html. Accessed February 24, 2004.

Houts P, Bachrach R, Witmer J, Tringali C, Bucher J, Localio R, 1998. "Using pictographs to enhance recall of spoken medical instructions," *Patient Education and Counseling*, 35:83–88.

Literacy in the information age: Final report of the international adult literacy survey, 2000. Statistics Canada. Available at http://www.statcan.ca/start.html. Accessed January 22, 2004.

Irvine C, 1999. *Health and Literacy Compendium*. Boston, MA: World Education, Inc. Available at http://www.worlded.org/publications.html. Accessed January 24, 2004.

Kirsch IS, Jungeblut A, Jenkins L, Kolstad A, 1993. *Adult literacy in America: A first look at the results of the national adult literacy survey*. National Center for Education Statistics. Washington, D.C.: U.S. Department of Education. Available at http://nces.ed.gov/naal. Accessed January 17, 2004.

McGee J, (ed).1999. *Writing and Designing Print Materials for Beneficiaries: A Guide for State Medicaid Agencies*. HCFA Publication Number 10145. Baltimore, MD: Centers for Medicare & Medicaid Services, U.S. Department of Health and Human Services. (A second edition is forthcoming in 2004. For ordering information, contact Jeanne McGee, McGee & Evers Consulting, Inc., Vancouver, Washington, 360-574-4744, jmcgee@pacifier.com).

National Institute for Literacy/LINCS. A large database of adult education and literacy resources in the United States including LINCSearch, MyLINCS, the Health & Literacy Special Collection/Compendium, and NIFL-Health (an online discussion group about health and literacy). Available at http://www.nifl.gov/lincs. Accessed January 24, 2004.

National Institute for Literacy, 1998. *The State of Literacy in America*. Washington, D.C.: National Institute for Literacy.

National Literacy and Health Program, 1998. *Easy Does It! Plain Language and Clear Verbal Communication.* Ontario, Canada: Canadian Public Health Association.

Nielsen-Bohlman L, Panzer AM, Kindig DA, 2004. *Health Literacy: A Prescription to End Confusion.* Institute of Medicine Washington, D.C.: The National Academies Press.

Osborne H, 2004. "In other words... adult learners and healthcare communication," *On Call* magazine, (3):16–17. Available at http://www.healthliteracy.com. Accessed May 15, 2004. Information is adapted and reprinted with permission of *On Call* magazine. *On Call* is published by BostonWorks, a division of the *Boston Globe.*

_____, 2002. *Partnering with Patients To Improve Health Outcomes.* Gaithersburg, MD: Aspen Publishers, Inc. Information is adapted and reprinted with the author's permission.

_____, 2000. *Overcoming Communication Barriers in Patient Education.* Gaithersburg, MD: Aspen Publishers, Inc. Information is adapted and reprinted with the author's permission.

_____, 1999a. "In other words... teaching with pictures," *On Call* magazine, 2(11):38–39. Available at http://www.healthliteracy.com. Accessed January 24, 2004. Information is adapted and reprinted with permission of *On Call* magazine. *On Call* is published by BostonWorks, a division of the *Boston Globe.*

_____, 1999b. "In other words... getting through... lives can depend on simplifying the written word," *On Call* magazine, 2(9):42–43. Available at http://www.healthliteracy.com. Accessed January 24, 2004. Information is adapted and reprinted with permission of *On Call* magazine. *On Call* is published by BostonWorks, a division of the *Boston Globe.*

Literacy

Media:
Videotapes,
Audiotapes,
CDs, and DVDs

Starting Points

Media such as videotapes, audiotapes, CDs, and DVDs are excellent tools to communicate health messages. Most everyone, including those with limited literacy or language skills, easily understands them. Media can usually be made accessible to those who have limited vision or are deaf or hard of hearing. As well, media can often be edited to reflect the age, culture, and interests of its viewing audience.

Media can be used throughout the continuum of care. For example, providers may show patients a video about an upcoming medical procedure or give a CD with instructions how to perform a self-care activity. Audiotapes may be used instead of, or as a supplement to, written materials. This can be particularly helpful for patients who have limited literacy or language skills. As well, media is often used as decision aids. For example, men diagnosed with prostate cancer may watch a video that presents unbiased information about treatment options, which helps them weigh decisions and make choices. (To learn more about decision aids, go to Decision Aids and Shared Decision-Making on page 39.)

Health-related media often combines emotional and educational content. For example, a video may include an inspirational first-person account of disease and recovery along with specific "how to" information. Many times, media presents information on sensitive or potentially embarrassing topics that people are reluctant to talk about.

Sometimes health facilities purchase media from publishing companies and health product catalogues; groups may create their own instead. This can be a low-budget audiotape of someone reading a health brochure aloud, or a professionally produced DVD geared for wide distribution. As well, with the publisher's permission and if the budget allows, groups may reproduce audio and videotapes for patients to take home. Whether on a large scale or small, the goal of health media is to present information in ways the intended audience can relate to, understand, and use.

Tom Kidder, at the Dartmouth-Hitchcock Medical Center in Lebanon, New Hampshire, produces many videos and other visual media. He talks about an especially moving and effective one he worked on about Amylateral Sclerosis (also know as ALS or Lou Gherig's disease). In this video, two people with ALS speak candidly about what it's like to live with the disease. A physician and a researcher talk about treatment options and outcomes. The patients, physician, and researcher together present a message that is realistic, yet optimistic. While they acknowledge the changes and losses that go along with ALS, their educational and inspirational message to viewers is to "enjoy the life you have and also prepare for inevitable changes."

Strategies, Ideas, and Suggestions

Content. As a rule, media does better with "soft" content like personal stories than it does with "hard" content such as complex data. One reason is that, unlike print materials, media is not apt to be viewed numerous times. Consider supplementing your media with written handouts. This way, viewers have an extra tool that reinforces learning, presents detailed data, and includes resources to learn more.

Organization. Media, like other teaching tools, should have just one message with a limited number (about three to five) of key points. These points should be organized from the viewers' perspective, such as presenting self-care instructions in order from first to last. Make the key points obvious by introducing them at the beginning, highlighting them throughout, and summarizing them at the end.

Consistency. Make sure the media's messages and words are consistent with actual practice. If they differ in significant ways, let viewers know. For example, an orthopedic clinic shows a video about lower back pain. The video, however, uses the term "long-term back pain" while the clinic staff says "chronic back pain." The staff can help by letting patients know that these terms mean essentially the same thing.

Tone. Media should engage viewers, with a balance of educational and emotional content. While most everyone appreciates a conversational and friendly tone, viewers may have trouble focusing if the media's tone is overly emotional and too sweet or too sad.

Culture. Your media should reflect the culture of its intended viewers, or at least be one they can accept and relate to. Teenagers, for example, may learn best when people in the video are of their age, talk like them, and wear clothing similar to their own.

Script. The narration portion of all media should be scripted (written) to be easy to listen to and understand. But don't try to script what patients and experts say; instead, include their actual words as "sound-bites" within the script. Generally, scripts should be in plain language using an active (not passive) voice, stating messages succinctly without extra words, and using terms people already know or explaining ones they need to learn. The most effective way to write and edit scripts is by reading the text aloud, always making sure it sounds like natural speech. (To learn more, go to Plain Language on page 179.)

Production values, pace, and pauses. Make sure the media's lighting and sound is of good quality and that the pacing is neither too fast nor too slow. While there are no rules about length, media should be short enough to keep viewers engaged and long enough to cover key points. Generally, this is between ten minutes and an hour. Allow time for viewers to ask questions and reflect on what they just learned. When you produce instructional media, add pauses after key points. When you show media, stop periodically and ask viewers for their questions and comments.

Technology. Technology is changing rapidly and yesterday's videotapes are being replaced by today's DVDs. Likewise, most audio programs are now on CD instead of tape. While these newer formats have many advantages (such as being interactive), make sure viewers have the necessary equipment to use them. Just in case, keep some older formats for those who do not have access to the latest technology.

Accessibility. Make sure your media is accessible to people of all abilities and languages. Include closed captions (words on the bottom of the screen) for those who cannot hear and descriptive audio (narration that describes all visuals) for people who cannot see. Accessible media also uses words and concepts that viewers know and avoids humor or clichés they might not understand.

Sponsorship. If the media you choose is sponsored by a particular company or manufacturer, alert viewers that it may represent just one point of view. As possible, supplement this media with unbiased information such as from federal agencies and national associations.

Timeliness. Make sure your media is accurate and up-to-date by reviewing it on a regular basis. Generally, videos and DVDs have a "shelf life" of about four to five years, though sometimes older ones (especially on basic topics) can be useful a few years longer.

Team. It takes a team to produce and select media that meets the needs of its audience.

- When creating media, this team should include: a production staff, including a producer, writer, camera operator, and editor (who may or may not be just one person); content experts, including health professionals, scientists, and educators; and intended users or patients and community members who ultimately will watch and listen to the media.

- When choosing media, the team should include at least the content experts and intended users. Whatever the composition of your team, listen carefully to the user's feedback and follow their suggestions to make needed changes. (To learn about feedback, go to Feedback: Interviews and Focus Groups on page 57.)

As a rule, media does better with "soft" content like personal stories than it does with "hard" content such as complex data.

Sources to Learn More

AMC Cancer Research Center, 1994. *Beyond the Brochure: Alternative Approaches to Effective Health Communication.* Center for Disease Control and Prevention. Available at http://www.cdc.gov/cancer/nbccedp. Accessed January 24, 2004.

Doak CC, Doak LG, Root JH, 1996. *Teaching Patients with Low Literacy Skills,* 2nd ed. Philadelphia, PA: J.B. Lippincott Company.

Fabel E, (date unavailable). *Assessing Health Education Videos: Guidelines for Health Educators and Trainers.* Boston, MA: World Education, Inc.

Films for the Humanities and Sciences. Available at http://www.films.com/Films_Home/Index.cfm?S=1. Accessed January 27, 2004.

Health Dialog. Available at http://www.healthdialog.com. Accessed January 24, 2004.

Osborne H, 2004. "In other words...helping patients make difficult decisions," *On Call* magazine, 7(4):16–17. Available at http://www.healthliteracy.com. Accessed May 15, 2004. Information is adapted and reprinted with permission of *On Call* magazine. *On Call* is published by BostonWorks, a division of the *Boston Globe.*

_____, 2002. *Partnering with Patients To Improve Health Outcomes.* Gaithersburg, MD: Aspen Publishers, Inc.

Medical-Legal Documents

Starting Points

Medical-legal documents, such as research informed consent documents, HIPAA (Health Insurance Portability and Accountability Act) materials, and institutional administrative or procedural forms, are notoriously difficult to read and understand. Many of these documents are written at college reading levels or beyond, and combine "legalese" and medical jargon known mostly to lawyers, administrators, and government bureaucrats. As well, medical-legal documents often include unfamiliar concepts such as "disclosure accounting" that average readers may not know or are not concerned about.

Beyond difficult words and concepts, many medical-legal forms have so much information that readers can easily get overwhelmed. For example, the U.S. Food and Drug Administration (FDA) requires that informed consent documents for research have eight basic elements plus six "when needed" ones. Some of these elements, such as descriptions of research drugs and their potential side effects, are quite technical. Adding the five to twelve items required for HIPAA, research consent forms can total 14 to 26 separate elements—a hefty amount of information for readers at all levels.

Admittedly, all medical-legal documents are not alike. Informed consent materials for research studies fall under FDA guidelines, which not only mandate the elements to include but also require that documents be written at a seventh-grade reading level or lower. Administrative and procedural documents, such as consent for hospital admission, are not governed by FDA standards. Generally, they only need to meet internal and accreditation standards, which may or may not stipulate reading level.

While most health providers do not write medical-legal documents, they need to be familiar enough with the wording and concepts to talk knowledgeably about them. Staff are trained how to do so at the Methodist Healthcare in Memphis, Tennessee. Research staff, for example, practice how to present materials to patients by first explaining these documents to their peers. Rather than simply repeating words in the consent form, staff must talk about concepts without looking at the document. This way, they gain the experience and confidence needed to communicate medical-legal information in ways patients can truly understand.

—From Rexann Pickering, PhD at
Methodist Healthcare in Memphis, TN

Strategies, Ideas, and Suggestions

Assessing readability. Readability formulas like the Fry and SMOG only measure the number of syllables in words and the number of words in sentences. These formulas do not assess whether readers comprehend concepts, especially abstract ones like risk and patient rights. Rather than relying solely on readability formulas, ask for feedback from people who represent your readers. Local literacy programs, for example, are often pleased to test documents and suggest ways to improve readability. (To learn more, go to Assessing Readability on page 13.)

Organization. While the content of medical-legal documents may be mandated (by in-house committees or outside agencies), the order in which information is presented is generally not. To improve readability, organize information from the reader's perspective. Start with a statement of personal relevance—why readers should know or care about this information. Then present the easier information first followed by more complex. You can also do this within each section by starting with general information and progressively adding more detail.

Plain language. Whenever possible, apply the principles of plain language to your medical-legal documents. Write in a conversational style using terms like "you" (the patient) and "we" (the organization or provider). As well, explain new concepts by putting them into context and giving examples. Design documents so that readers can easily find the information they need. One way to do this is by having headers that clearly indicate what each section is about.

Whenever possible, use common words that people already know. This means using words like "choice" instead of "alternative" and "tell us" rather than "notify." To make this task easier in subsequent documents, you might want to create an in-house glossary of acceptable substitute words. An excellent place to start is with the "Thesaurus of Plain Language Words and Phrases for HIPAA Notices of Privacy Practices," which is available at http://www.hrsa. gov/language.htm.

Concepts, categories, and value judgments. Another reason that medical-legal documents are hard to understand is because they include a lot of concept, category, and value judgment words.

- "Concept" refers to general or abstract ideas like "double-blind study" or "screening process."
- "Category" words are groups of similar items like "adverse reactions" or "regulatory authorities."
- "Value judgments" are amounts or thresholds like "minor inconvenience" or "reasonable effort."

To make these terms clear, include definitions or examples. For instance, you could write "you will need a blood test every month" instead of "you will have regular blood tests" (Hochhauser, 2003).

Layout and visuals. Just because medical-legal documents are important doesn't mean they have to be unattractive. Consider adding simple line drawings or culturally appropriate images to help readers understand. You can also draw attention to important pieces of information by drawing arrows or putting boxes and circles around them. Although visuals may increase the length of documents, their benefits in improving readability can make this trade-off worthwhile.

Actions. Encourage people not only to read documents but also to take action. Provide spaces below key content areas with directions to "write any questions you have about what you just read." Also, ask readers to circle any words they do not know the meaning of or do not fully understand. This way, you can be more aware of words and concepts to discuss with patients in greater detail.

Easy-to-read summary. As a health professional, your job is to present information that is honest and complete yet not overwhelming. For some types of forms, you can help by writing companion easier-to-read summaries. My dentist, for example, has a one-page summary of HIPAA information stapled on top of the more complex regulations. When I asked how patients react, the office staff said that nearly all patients read only the summary and not the full document.

Summaries, however, cannot be used as easily in the research arena. Indeed, they must have Institutional Review Board (IRB) approval and prospective research subjects need to sign both the original document and the summary.

Environment. Help patients understand medical-legal documents by creating an environment in which they can comfortably ask for help and have sufficient time to read and process information. Make sure, as well, that the environment feels private and is secure. For example, if you ask patients to write their social security numbers on a form, shred any copies they might discard because of errors. As well, be sensitive to people's emotional states. For sure, it is difficult to concentrate on complex medical-legal information when people are sick, stressed, or anxious about upcoming treatments or procedures.

A team approach. It takes a team to write understandable medical-legal documents. At a minimum, this team should include subject-matter experts, writers, and readers. Subject-matter experts include scientists, health providers, lawyers, and administrators who are responsible for the content. Writers need to understand the concepts and also be skilled in plain language. Readers should represent the intended audience in terms of literacy, language, age, and culture. Working as a team, you can indeed write medical-legal documents that readers will understand.

Help patients understand medical-legal documents by creating an environment in which they can comfortably ask for help and have sufficient time to read and process information.

Sources to Learn More

Brandes WL ed., 1996. *Literacy, Health, and the Law: An Exploration of the Law and the Plight of Marginal Reader Within the Healthcare System.* Philadelphia, PA: Health Promotion Council of Southeastern Pennsylvania, Inc.

Hochhauser M, 2003. Why patients won't understand their HIPAA privacy notices. Available at the Privacy Rights Clearinghouse website, http://www.privacyrights.org/ar/HIPAA-Readability.htm. Accessed January 20, 2004.

_____, 2003. "Concepts, categories, and value judgments in informed consent forms," *IRB: Ethics & Human Research*, 25(5):7–10.

Osborne H, 2001. "In other words...how the new HIPAA regulations affect healthcare communication," *On Call* magazine, 4(7):42–43. Available at http://www.healthliteracy.com. Accessed January 22, 2004. Information is adapted and reprinted with permission of *On Call* magazine. *On Call* is published by BostonWorks, a division of the *Boston Globe*.

_____, 1999. "In other words...advance directives...helping people understand," *On Call* magazine, 2(6):50–51. Available at http://www.healthliteracy.com. Accessed January 22, 2004. Information is adapted and reprinted with permission of *On Call* magazine. *On Call* is published by BostonWorks, a division of the *Boston Globe*.

Paasche-Orlow MK, Taylor HA, Brancati FL, 2003. "Readability standards for informed-consent forms as compared with actual readability," *New England Journal of Medicine*, 348(8):721–726.

Plain Language Principles and Thesaurus for Making HIPAA Privacy Notices More Readable, HRSA of the U.S. Department of Health and Human Services, Washington, D.C. Available at http://www.hrsa.gov/language.htm. Accessed January 22, 2004.

Metaphors and Analogies

Starting Points

Metaphors, also know as analogies, help people understand unfamiliar words, terms, and concepts by linking them to examples they are already acquainted with. Given the abundance of new health information for which patients have no framework to understand, metaphors can indeed be very useful communication tools.

Metaphors are short, clear, visual, and illustrative ways to enhance understanding. They generally include three components:

- the unfamiliar information or "target,"
- a familiar example or "analog," and
- a connecter word such as "like" or "as."

Here are some examples of metaphors that answer the question, "Why don't we use antibiotics for colds, acute bronchitis, and other viral illnesses?"

You don't use bug spray to kill weeds in your lawn.

Using antibiotics for viruses is like using a large net to catch minnows. They just go through the holes.

Using antibiotics for viruses is like putting gas in your gas tank if your battery is dead.

Treating a cold with antibiotics is like using an umbrella to stay warm in winter. It just doesn't work and when it starts to rain, your umbrella might be worn out.

—From the Altoona List of Medical Analogies
found at www.altoonafp.org/analogies

Strategies, Ideas, and Suggestions

Determine when to use a metaphor. Some healthcare concepts are straight forward and a simple explanation is sufficient. Save metaphors for those times when you are teaching something that is unfamiliar or hard to understand. For example, you might use a metaphor to explain a new diagnosis like emphysema but not for a commonly understood condition like the flu.

Use words, terms, and examples that people know. To be effective, the person you are speaking with needs to know what your analog (example) means. For instance, saying "getting a vaccination is like installing anti-virus software" may have meaning to someone familiar with computers. But if the person prefers camping to computing, you might instead say "getting a vaccine is like putting on bug spray before going in the woods."

Explain the metaphor. Metaphors by themselves are seldom sufficient. After you use one, follow up with a fuller explanation. If you say "an aneurysm is like a bulge in a garden hose," explain how these concepts are alike by saying, "The bigger the bulge, the thinner the wall and the more likely it will burst."

Acknowledge limitations of your metaphor, as well. In this instance you might say how aneurysms happen only in certain parts of the body while garden hoses can get bulges most everywhere.

Move beyond the metaphor. After you confirm that a patient understands the metaphor, transition to the correct medical terminology. In the example above about an aneurysm, this means teaching important terms like "aortic aneurysm" and "cerebral aneurysm."

Confirm understanding. Metaphors aren't always obvious nor are they necessarily understood in the way you intend. Sometimes they add to confusion. A physician was explaining to his patient that her heart "is like a pump." He assumed that, since the patient lived in a rural area, she would certainly understand the metaphor. While the patient smiled and nodded politely, it wasn't until several visits later that she told her doctor that she had no idea how pumps work. Knowing this, the physician explained her cardiac condition in another way. As with all forms of health communication, make sure that patients truly understand.

Metaphors can be very helpful in health communication because there is an abundance of new terms that patients need to know yet have no framework to understand.

Sources to Learn More

The Altoona List of Medical Analogies. Available at http://www.altoonafp.org/analogies.htm. Accessed January 26, 2004.

Osborne H, 2003. "In other words...it's like what you already know...using analogies to help patients understand," *On Call* magazine, 6(1):16–17. Available at http://www.healthliteracy.com. Accessed January 25, 2004. Information is adapted and reprinted with permission of *On Call* magazine. *On Call* is published by BostonWorks, a division of the *Boston Globe*.

Numbers

Starting Points

To understand most health information, people need a working knowledge of numbers. They must understand and use numbers to make sense of risk data, to select healthy foods by reading nutrition labels, to calculate if they have enough pills, to estimate costs and figure budgets, and to rate satisfaction or pain on scales from one to ten. Without a working knowledge of numbers, people must rely on others to help them with these tasks.

But numbers are difficult for many people. The National Adult Literacy Survey shows that 47% of the adults in the United States have trouble with quantitative literacy, defined as "the knowledge and skills required to apply arithmetic operations, alone or sequentially, [or] using numbers embedded in printed materials"(Kirsch, et al., 1993). Older adults tend to have even greater difficulty. The same study found that more than 70% of people aged 60 and over have trouble with calculations or with understanding tables and graphs (Brown, et al., 1996).

People of all ages find numbers difficult for a variety of reasons. Some find that big numbers blend together, "A million, billion, trillion—what's the difference?" (Best, 2001). Others struggle with small numbers expressed as percents, decimals, or fractions. People may not know how to interpret charts, tables, graphs, and other visual displays of data. Or they may lack the math skills needed to accurately add, subtract, multiply, or divide. Unlike literacy, trouble with understanding numbers is seldom a source of shame. In fact, people may proudly boast, "I don't do numbers."

In healthcare today, people need a working knowledge of numbers. This includes familiarity with fractions and decimal points needed to adjust medication or interpret temperature readings. It also includes being able to do calculations necessary for recipes or paying bills. Here are two examples of common difficulties.

Decimal numbers. Most people handle small whole numbers effectively, but the decimal point and what it indicates often gets ignored. For example, it's easy for most people to see that a 104 degree temperature is 2 degrees higher than a 102 degree temperature. But there is less certainty about the relative difference between 100.4 degrees and 102 degrees.

Calculations. Certain "tried and true" steps like how to line up numbers for calculations fall apart with decimals. When adding 15 + 6, the numbers must line up on the right—with the 6 below the 5.

$$\begin{array}{r} 15 \\ +\ 6 \\ \hline 21 \end{array}$$

But when adding 1.5 + 6, the rule changes and the numbers now need to line up on the left—with the 6 below the 1.

$$\begin{array}{r} 1.5 \\ +\ 6 \\ \hline 7.5 \end{array}$$

But when adding 1.5 +.6, the numbers again need to line up on the right—with the 6 below the 5.

$$
\begin{array}{r}
1.5 \\
+\ .6 \\
\hline
2.1
\end{array}
$$

Calculations like these may be easy for some people. But to patients who have not used math in many years or perhaps never had strong math skills, accurate calculations can be nearly impossible. In healthcare today, the cost of miscalculation can be high, especially when it leads to medication or interpretation errors.

—From Mary Jane Schmitt and Martha Merson of the EMPower Project at Technical Education Research Centers (TERC) in Cambridge, MA

Strategies, Ideas, and Suggestions

People make their own meaning of numbers. While it's tempting to assume that everyone understands numbers the same way, it is not necessarily so. Cholesterol measurements, for example, seem straightforward and scientific. While people may boast or commiserate about their cholesterol, their numbers have little meaning when taken out of context. For instance, one person's cholesterol of 220 may indicate progress while another person's 220 may be of medical concern. To help patients make sense of these numbers, give additional information such as high and low parameters or what their cholesterol numbers were last year.

Math. Be sensitive to the fact that patients may have difficulty with even "simple" math calculations. For example, a person may need to add the number of fat grams he or she eats each day or instead divide a recipe in half. As I write this, I'm looking at the nutrition label on a cereal box. It says that each serving size is 1⅓ cups and there are 9 servings per container. For sure, calculating anything useful from these numbers boggles my mind.

Providers can help by showing patients how to figure math problems. Instead of just assuming their calculations are correct, double-check patients math and confirm the accuracy of their answers.

Percents, fractions, decimals. To understand percents, fractions, and decimals, people need to consider two separate numeric elements and the relationship between them. This is not always easy or intuitive. For example, when comparing ⅓ to ½, some people may incorrectly figure that since 3 is a bigger number than 2 that ⅓ is therefore bigger than ½.

Recipes and other types of nutrition information often use fractions like these. To help patients better understand, show a picture or demonstrate with measuring cups what these fractions really mean.

Risk data. Patients need to understand risks and benefits before they consent to new procedures or protocols. But risk data is notoriously difficult to explain and understand, due in part to number-based concepts that may be included like frequency, probability, and time.

For example, providers may present data in terms of "relative risk" which is a ratio or percentage like "40% of people who…," or "absolute risk" that is an actual number such as "4 out of 10 people…." In addition, providers may frame risk in positive terms such as "95% of people have…" or negative terms like "5% of people don't have…." As well, providers may talk about populations, "2,700 out of 10,000 people" while patients may just want to know "what will happen to me?"

Patients may incorrectly assume that all risk data is accurate and relevant. Encourage patients to think critically when they hear statistics like "1 in 7 people will get (x) disease." Ask them to consider where this number comes from, how the data was collected, and whether the number is apt to change over time. As well, ask patients to find out if people in this study are similar to them in terms of age, gender, risk factors, and health status. (To learn more, go to Risk Communication on page 193.)

Words and numbers. Words sometimes serve as shorthand for numbers. Informed consent documents, for example, may mention "common," "uncommon," and "rare" risks. While a researcher may intend "common" to mean a risk affecting about 10% of subjects, patients may instead assume that a "common" risk affects most everyone. To clarify these concepts, use both numbers and words such as: "A common risk affects about 1 out of 10 people."

Visual displays of numbers. Numbers can be displayed in many ways including tables, graphs, pie charts, risk ladders, and histograms. While it almost certainly helps to use visuals to show number-based concepts, researchers are not in agreement about which type of visuals works best.

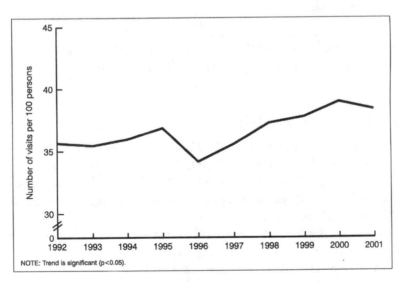

NOTE: Trend is significant (p<0.05).

Figure 1.1. A graph showing trends in emergency department visit rates: United States, 1992–2001.

Other ways to express numbers. You're only limited by your imagination and creativity. Here are some other ways to help people understand numbers:

- Compare numbers to known quantities. For example, "You can lift up to 5 pounds—about the same weight as a bag of flour."

- Give analogies. You could say, "The chance of you getting (x) disease is like you catching a fly ball at Fenway Park."

- Show pictures. Perhaps include illustrations of three drinking glasses—one that is ¼ full, another ½, full, and the third ¾ full.

- Use real objects. Instead of just talking about portion size, show people what 4 ounces of chicken really looks like.

Confirm understanding. Make sure patients truly understand numbers and data. You might, for example, ask patients to tell you how they will explain number-based information to a friend or family member. And make sure you truly understand as well. Just because you are a health provider does not make you immune from number trouble.

Unlike literacy, trouble with understanding numbers is seldom a source of shame. In fact, people may proudly boast, "I don't do numbers."

Sources to Learn More

Best J, 2001. *Damned Lies and Statistics: Untangling Numbers from the Media, Politicians, and Activists.* Berkeley, CA: University of California Press.

Brown H, Prisuta R, Jacobs B, Campbell A, 1996. *Literacy of Older Adults in America.* National Center for Education Statistics. Washington, D.C.: U.S. Department of Education.

Centre for Environmental Research and Training, (date unavailable). *Risk literacy and the public.* University of Birmingham, Available at http://www.doh.gov.uk/pointers.htm. Accessed January 25, 2004.

Edwards A, Elwyn G, Mulley A, 2002. "Explaining risks: Turning numerical data into meaningful pictures," *BMJ*, 324:827–830.

Gigerenzer G, Edwards A, 2003. Simple tools for understanding risks: From innumeracy to insight, *British Medical Journal*, 327:741–744.

Hochhauser M, 2003. "Subject recruitment and informed consent," *Applied Clinical Trials Supplement*, November:10–13.

Innumeracy.com. Available at http://innumeracy.com. Accessed January 25, 2004.

Kertesz L, 2003. The numbers behind the news, *Healthplan*, 44(5).

Kirsch I, Jungeblut A, Jenkins L, Kolstad A, 1993. *Adult Literacy in America*. Washington, D.C.: National Center for Education Statistics.

Lipkus IM, Hollands JG, 1999. "The visual communication of risk," *Journal of the National Cancer Institute*, Monograph 25:149–163.

TERC, Science and Math Learning, EMPower Project. Available at http://empower.terc.edu. Accessed January 25, 2004.

Objects and Models

Starting Points

Health information is commonly communicated in speaking and writing. While these methods often work well, some people (myself included) learn better when we can see, touch, manipulate, or otherwise interact with actual objects or simulated models.

Objects and models give clear images of what providers are talking about. They can be used to introduce new ideas or to reinforce familiar concepts. Sometimes, objects and models add an extra element of intrigue or excitement. For example, a doll that simulates cigarette smoking and has collection tube "lungs" can help people clearly see what nicotine and tar buildup actually looks like.

While realistic, objects and models need not be exact replicas of the concepts they are demonstrating. Sometimes they are intentionally exaggerated to attract attention to important health messages. The Colossal Colon is an example.

The Colossal Colon is a 40-foot long, 4-foot high replica of a human colon. Visitors who crawl through the colon or look through the viewing windows, will see healthy colon tissue, colon disease, polyps and various stages of colon cancer. The Colossal Colon was modeled after a real colon taken from colonoscopy film footage and is extremely lifelike. Going through the colon, visitors not only gain a general understanding of the digestive system (a part of their body they may not know a lot about), but also learn specifically about colorectal prevention, screening, and treatment.

In just one year, more than 60,000 people in 20 United States cities visited the Colossal Colon. Young children, senior citizens, and people of all ages in between not only found this exhibit funny and fun but also left with a much greater understanding about colorectal cancer. As one organizer said, "Grab people's attention and then they'll pay attention and learn."

—From Shanna Duncan of the Cancer Research and
Prevention Foundation

Figure 1.1. The Colossal colon helps people learn about colon cancer. *Source:* http://www.preventcancer.org/colossalcolon/Tour/what_colon.htm. Used with permission from the Cancer Research and Prevention Foundation.

Strategies, Ideas, and Suggestions

Audience. Models and objects can be helpful for people of all ages, abilities, disabilities, literacy levels, languages, and cultures. They can even work well with people who are traditionally squeamish about their body and bodily functions. A surgeon, for example, can use a model of the gall bladder to show patients why theirs must be removed.

Simulated models. Lifelike models can be made from plastic, wood, rubber, or even food such as chocolate or gelatin. They provide hands-on learning opportunities that are educational but not scary or gory. A chiropractor, for example, can demonstrate on a model how she will manipulate the patient's spine. As well, patients can use models to practice self-injections or breast self-examinations. Make sure, however, that patients can perform these procedures as well on themselves as they do on the model.

Actual objects. Sometimes, perhaps due to budget considerations, you might want to use actual objects instead of simulated models. This may mean demonstrating food portion size by showing a four-ounce serving of chicken or using a serving spoon to measure out a half-cup portion of rice. You can also create scrapbooks with pictures of suggested items. When talking about nutrition, you can include clippings from supermarket advertisements as well as actual food labels that patients can take to the grocery store. This way, even people with limited reading skills need only match the labels to the actual products they want to buy.

Actual medicine bottles and medical devices can work equally well. For example, you could use a prescription bottle to explain what the different labels mean. Or you can demonstrate how to use a bronchodilator and have the patient try it as well.

Use a combination of teaching techniques. You might find that patients learn best when you use several teaching tools including models, objects, illustrations, demonstrations, opportunities for

Objects and Models

practice, and written handouts. When teaching about cholesterol, for example, you might begin with an illustration of what cholesterol looks like in the body. Then you could show some foods (real or simulated) and discuss the amount of fat, sugar, and salt in them. And, if you want to make the point even more clear, pass around simulated replicas of human fat that people can look at and touch. At this point, patients are most likely very ready to learn how to lower their cholesterol levels.

Memorable teaching tools. Sometimes, people understand and remember concepts because the teaching tools are so unexpected. Local police departments, for example, sometimes make gelatin molds that look like human brains. When they run bicycle safety programs for school children, these "gelatin brains" make clear why the students should wear bicycle helmets. Indeed, objects and models can provide memorable tools for learning.

Models and objects can be helpful for people of all ages, abilities, disabilities, literacy levels, languages, and cultures.

Sources to Learn More

Anatomical Chart Company offers a wide range of anatomical models, training aids, and posters. Available at 1-800-621-7500 and http://anatomical.com. Accessed January 25, 2004.

Cancer Research and Prevention Foundation, available at http://www.prevent-cancer.org. Accessed January 25, 2004.

Colossal Colon Tour. Available at http://www.preventcancer.org/colossalcolon/Tour/what_colon.htm Accessed January 25, 2004.

Osborne H, 2002. "In other words...getting formal...finding the teaching tools you need at a price your organization can afford," *On Call* magazine, 5(7):38–39. Available at http://www.healthliteracy.com. Accessed January 22, 2004. Information is adapted and reprinted with permission of *On Call* magazine. *On Call* is published by BostonWorks, a division of the *Boston Globe*.

Older Adults

Starting Points

Older adults, aged 65 years and over, are a significant and ever-increasing percentage of the United States population. The fastest growing segment is those who are 85 years and above. Collectively, older adults are a remarkably diverse group. People in their mid-60s are apt to have far different needs and abilities than those who are two, three, or more decades older.

Despite individual differences, as people age they are likely to be diagnosed with illnesses that result in disabilities. Consequently, people may need assistance with daily living tasks including dressing, bathing, preparing meals, and taking medication. Older adults (and their caretakers, if any) need to understand how to accomplish these tasks, to manage symptoms and side effects, and to recognize and take appropriate action in emergencies.

Learning this information can be difficult, due in part to the fact that health information has many unfamiliar words, concepts, instructions, and devices. Also, many older adults have primary diseases or complications from chronic illnesses that may impair their physical, cognitive, or sensory skills. The medications that people take (including prescribed, over the counter, and home remedies) can interfere with their alertness and attention span. Emotional issues, too, can affect older adults. It is indeed hard for a person to concentrate when dealing with stresses like moving, losing family members and friends, or going from being the family caregiver to the person being taken care of.

In addition, many older adults have trouble reading. A large-scale literacy survey found that more than 70 percent of older adults have significant difficulty reading complex text and even more struggle to understand and complete forms and documents (Brown, et al., 1996). While no one knows for sure why this is so, there are hypotheses. One is that many older adults dropped out of school before graduation and so never acquired strong reading skills. Another is that many older adults watch TV or listen to the radio rather than read, and so their reading skills have declined from disuse. Another reason may be that many older adults have not been in the workforce recently (or ever) and are not used to filling out forms or using tables and charts with number-based information. With all these factors, it is no wonder that older adults can have trouble with medical instructions.

"Mrs. Smith" is an 84-year-old woman who lives alone. She comes to her appointment complaining of shortness of breath. To make an accurate diagnosis, the nurse practitioner listens to Mrs. Smith's lungs and orders follow-up tests. The nurse asks Mrs. Smith to go to the seventh floor to have her blood drawn, to go to the second floor for a chest X-ray, and to return to her office before going to the pharmacy. Mrs. Smith cheerfully agrees. But, as the nurse later learns, Mrs. Smith leaves the facility soon after her blood is drawn. While there may be many reasons why she does not follow through, a likely reason is that Mrs. Smith did not understand or could not remember all four of the nurse's instructions.

Strategies, Ideas, and Suggestions

Positive and supportive approach. Create "shame-free" learning environments where older adults can comfortably acknowledge when they do and do not understand. Let patients who seem confused know they are not the only ones having trouble—that many people find it hard to learn new health information. Another way is for staff or volunteers to offer assistance with filling out paperwork or finding unfamiliar locations.

Environment. Make sure that your environment is conducive to learning and good communication. Have large, readable signs that clearly inform people where they are. Make sure to have well-lit rooms, halls, and quiet, private spaces in which to meet and talk.

Environments should also be accessible to people with disabilities. Have railings on the wall for people to hold on to and straight-backed chairs they can easily get into and out of. Make sure that the type on printed materials is not only large enough but also sufficiently dark for people to see—sometimes this is a problem with duplicate or reproduced copies. As well, don't rely just on color to help people navigate your environment. While color-coded arrows can be very helpful for some, they may be of no use to people who are blind or visually impaired.

Learning and teaching. Gerogogy is a model of teaching older adults. It builds on the principles of adult learning theory and includes teaching interventions designed to compensate for physical, sensory, and cognitive deficits (Hayes, 1998). Gerogogy includes:

- Scheduling teaching for when older adults have sufficient energy. For example, this may mean scheduling several brief teaching sessions rather than a single lengthy one.

- Organizing health messages from the patient's perspective and tying new information to past experiences.

Older Adults

- Limiting your message to a few (seven or less) key points. As necessary, dividing larger amounts of information into smaller modules.

- Adjusting the teaching pace so that you are neither going so slow that patients are bored nor so fast that they cannot keep up with you. Beyond directly asking, you may pick up clues about pace by noticing people's body language or asking questions to find out how much they are learning.

- Teaching instructions one step at a time, presenting information as concretely as possible, and omitting extraneous facts that may be confusing.

- Demonstrating, not just describing, procedures and encouraging older adults to practice alongside you.

- Being concrete and specific, not just saying "get some exercise" but instead "go for three ten-minute walks every day."

- Repeating the most important points throughout the teaching session, concluding with a short summary, and alerting patients to what they can expect next.

Spoken information. Speak slowly, clearly, and concisely, and introduce just one new concept at a time. Use "living room language" with words that older adults know and are comfortable with. As well, pay attention to nonverbal communication—both yours and the patient's. Throughout your conversation, pause periodically for patients' questions and to confirm understanding.

Reading and writing. Informally assess patient's reading skills by paying attention to clues of literacy problems such as when people repeatedly "forget" their eyeglasses. Rather than ask people if they can read, you might ask how far they went in school—but appreciate that the last grade completed does not necessarily indicate reading ability. In fact, most people read at least two to three grade levels lower than their last completed year of school. (To learn more about literacy, go to Literacy: Communicating with People Who Do Not Read or Read Well on page 131.)

Provide older adults with printed materials that are written in plain language and have examples and illustrations they can understand and relate to. The best way to know if written materials meet the needs of readers is to ask. (To learn more about choosing materials, go to Choosing, Adapting, and Reviewing Teaching Materials on page 27.)

Provide multiple ways for people to learn. Show (do not just tell) people about health information. For example, supplement spoken and written information with pictographs and illustrations, media including videotapes, or demonstrations using real objects or simulated models. You can also help older adults learn by sharing stories—yours or theirs—to help them connect with health information in a more personal way. (To learn more about stories, go to Stories and Narratives on page 205.)

Help patients participate. Encourage older patients to bring lists of their concerns and questions to appointments. When you meet, discuss a patient's goals and confidence in managing her or his illness. Periodically ask for questions but be sensitive to the fact that many older adults were brought up to not question medical professionals and may be reluctant or unwilling to do so. (To learn more about helping people prepare for and participate in appointments, go to Helping Patients Prepare For and Participate in Healthcare on page 85.)

Help patients remember. Call patients ahead of time to remind them of appointments and afterwards to reinforce instructions and answer unanswered questions. Other ways to help patients remember are by sending reminder postcards, suggesting they keep notebooks with personal health information, and recommending pillboxes or other adherence aids. Rather than assuming that people know how to use these aids, demonstrate first such as by filling a pillbox with a week's worth of medicine. (To learn more about helping patients remember and follow medical information, go to Helping Patients Remember and Follow Medical Instructions on page 93.)

Family members and friends. Encourage patients to invite a trusted friend or family member to accompany them to appointments. This way, older adults not only learn in the company of people they find supportive but also have a second pair of "eyes and ears" to reinforce and clarify information after appointments are over.

Verify understanding. Regardless of age, make sure that patients understand the information you are communicating. You can do this by asking relevant and specific open-ended questions such as, "Some people get dizzy after they take this medicine. If this happens, what will you do?"

There are vast differences among older adults. People in their mid-60s are apt to have far different needs and abilities than those who are two, three, or more decades older.

Sources to Learn More

Bonnel WB, 1999. "Patient teaching for older adults and families in the long-term care setting," *Journal of Nurses in Staff Development*, 15(2):75–77.

Brown H, Prisuta R, Jacobs B, Campbell A, 1996. *Literacy of Older Adults in America*. National Center for Education Statistics. Washington, D.C.: U.S. Department of Education.

Department of Health and Human Services, Administration on Aging, 2002. A profile of older Americans. Available at http://www.aoa.gov/prof/Statistics/profile/12_pf.asp. Accessed January 25, 2004.

Hayes KS, 1998. "Randomized trial of gerogogy-based medication instruction in the emergency department," *Nursing Research*, 47(4):211–218.

Jackson R, Davis, T, Murphy P, Bairnsfather L, George, R, 1994. "Reading deficiencies in older patients," *The American Journal of the Medical Sciences*, 308(2).

Murphy P, Davis T, Jackson R, Decker B, Long S, 1993. "Effects of literacy on health care of the aged: Implications for health professionals," *Educational Gerontology*, 19:311–316.

National Literacy and Health Program, 1998. *Working with Low-literacy Seniors: Practical Strategies for Health Providers.* Ontario, Canada: Canadian Public Health Association.

Osborne H, 2002. "In other words…making it work…selecting healthcare brochures for older adults," *On Call* magazine, 5(10):16–17. Available at http://www.healthliteracy.com. Accessed January 18, 2004. Information is adapted and reprinted with permission of *On Call* magazine. *On Call* is published by BostonWorks, a division of the *Boston Globe.*

_____, 2001. "In other words…mind what you say…speaking with and listening to older adults," *On Call* magazine, 4(6):50–52. Available at http://www.healthliteracy.com. Accessed January 18, 2004. Information is adapted and reprinted with permission of *On Call* magazine. *On Call* is published by BostonWorks, a division of the *Boston Globe.*

_____, 2000. *Overcoming Communication Barriers in Patient Education.* Gaithersburg, MD: Aspen Publishers, Inc. Information is adapted and reprinted with the author's permission.

_____, 1999. "In other words…literacy and the older adult," *On Call* magazine, 2(10):42–43. Available at http://www.healthliteracy.com. Accessed January 18, 2004. Information is adapted and reprinted with permission of *On Call* magazine. *On Call* is published by BostonWorks, a division of the *Boston Globe.*

Osborne H, Hochhauser M, 1999. "Readability and comprehension of the introduction to the Massachusetts healthcare proxy," *Hospital Topics,* 77(4):4–6. Available at www.healthliteracy.com. Accessed January 18, 2004.

Pearson, M, Wessman J, 1996. "Gerogogy," *Home Healthcare Nurse,* 14(8):632–636.

Stevens B, 2003. "How seniors learn," *Issue Brief.* Center for Medicare Education, 4(9). Available at www.MedicareEd.org. Accessed January 25, 2004.

Older Adults

Pictographs

Starting Points

Pictographs are simple line drawings that represent ideas or actions. They are distinct from other types of visuals in that they needn't be (and often aren't) magnificent works of art. In fact, pictographs can simply be stick figures or impromptu sketches that just give visual cues. From cave paintings to airport signage, pictographs have been used throughout the ages to show concepts that are hard to put into words. They are equally effective in healthcare.

Many people appreciate pictographs and other visual tools to help them understand new or complicated health information. Peter Houts, PhD and his colleagues found that pictographs help people learn and recall. In a research study, they showed pictographs and explained them to adults who read at less than a fifth-grade level. Looking at the pictographs a month later, 71% of the people could accurately recall (cued recall) the meaning of these pictographs (Houts, et al., 2001). Given that many us have trouble remembering what we ate for lunch a few hours ago, this is a remarkable finding indeed.

An example from my own experience follows:

Pictographs can help learners of all abilities. Several years ago, I had a mole removed from my toe and the biopsy showed it had spread through several layers of skin. Even though I'm a literate, well-educated health professional, I had trouble comprehending what my doctor was explaining. To help, she drew a quick sketch of my mole on the white paper from the examining table. What a relief to see (and not just hear) that my mole wasn't really all that bad.

Strategies, Ideas, and Suggestions

Draw pictographs or use ones that others have created. Pictographs can be spontaneous, like the impromptu drawing of my mole. Or pictographs can be doodles or sketches on already-drawn diagrams. For example, an orthopedic surgeon who sees a lot of patients for knee surgery may start with a pre-printed sheet of basic knee anatomy and add his own markings to make the drawing personal before he gives it to each patient.

Find out how people like to learn. Ask (rather than assume) how people like to learn. You might do this by giving options like "How do you like to learn—by looking at pictures, reading booklets, or talking with someone?" While many people enjoy and learn from pictographs, be sensitive to the fact that some might find them childish or unappealing. You might be able to soften this with a dose of humor about your budding second career as an artist.

Keep pictographs simple. When you draw, include only the most important elements or actions and omit non-essential details. For example, when the doctor drew the picture of my mole she only included enough detail to show how far the mole had spread and not all of my foot's anatomy.

Supplement pictographs. Pictographs are not necessarily self-evident. Talk aloud as you draw. Then add a simply worded phrase or sentence beneath each one to make its meaning clear. This combination of drawing, talking, and writing helps most everyone to understand and remember.

Pictographs are also excellent for showing step-by-step instructions—especially when you number each step and add boxes for people to check when they complete each action.

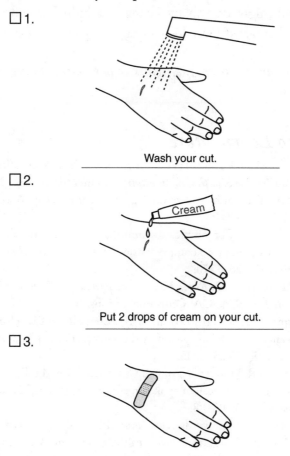

☐1.

Wash your cut.

☐2.

Put 2 drops of cream on your cut.

☐3.

Put a bandage on your cut.

Give your pictograph away. Your pictographs—even those that look a lot like scribbles—may be important to the patients with whom you are working. Ask patients if they'd like to keep your drawing. When they do, add a few words beneath so everyone who sees the pictograph will understand its meaning.

Encourage patients to draw. Just as you have trouble putting some ideas into words, patients may also find it difficult to express what they want to say. Encourage patients to draw pictures for you and make it easy by having pads of paper and colored pencils or markers nearby.

Confirm understanding. Just like all other forms of communication, make sure that the person you are with fully understands. With pictographs, you might do this by saying in a light-hearted way, "Let's see how good an artist I am. What does this picture mean to you?"

Pictographs can simply be stick figures or impromptu sketches that give just visual cues.

Sources to Learn More

AMC Cancer Research Center, 1994. *Beyond the Brochure: Alternative Approaches to Effective Health Communication.* Center for Disease Control and Prevention. Available at http://www.cdc.gov/cancer/nbccedp. Accessed January 24, 2004.

Delp C, Jones J, 1996. "Communicating information to patients: The use of cartoon illustrations to improve comprehension of instructions," *Academic Emergency Medicine,* 3(3):264–270.

Hanks K, Belliston L, 1990. *Rapid Viz: A New Method for the Rapid Visualization of Ideas.* Menlo Park, CA: Crisp Publications, Inc.

Houts P, Witmer J, Egeth HE, Loscalzo MJ, Zabora JR, 2001. "Using pictographs to enhance recall of spoken medical instructions II," *Patient Education and Counseling,* 43:231–242.

Houts P, Bachrach R, Witmer J, Tringali C, Bucher J, Localio R, 1998. "Using pictographs to enhance recall of spoken medical instructions," *Patient Education and Counseling,* 35:83–88.

Osborne H, 1999. "In other words...teaching with pictures," *On Call* magazine, 2(11):38–39. Available at http://www.healthliteracy.com. Accessed January 24, 2004. Information is adapted and reprinted with permission of *On Call* magazine. *On Call* is published by BostonWorks, a division of the *Boston Globe.*

Sonneman MR, 1997. *Beyond Words: A Guide to Drawing Out Ideas.* Berkeley, CA: Ten Speed Press.

Plain Language

Starting Points

Plain language (or "plain English") helps everyone—not just readers who have limited literacy or language skills. According to the United States Plain Language Action and Information Network (PLAIN), plain language is a way of writing that "is visually inviting, logically organized, and understandable on the first reading."

Plain language uses organization, words, sentences, tone, layout, graphics, and interaction to help make written materials both more appealing and easier to read. Plain language also means being as concise as possible. Admittedly, it is sometimes hard to decide which information to include or omit. You can make these decisions easier by working with a team of content experts and readers. Together, you can decide what to present in this booklet and what to delete or include in another publication.

Admittedly, it is difficult to demonstrate all of the plain language principles in a short passage that is taken out of context.

Antacids (indigestion medicine): Unless you have high blood pressure or another disorder that requires you to cut down on salt, an occasional antacid for stomach upset shouldn't hurt.	Antacid is medicine for indigestion (feeling sick after you eat). Most people can take antacids. But do not take antacids if you have high blood pressure or need to cut down on salt.
Before plain language	After plain language

Figure 1.1. A before and after example of plain language. Before sentences are from a health brochure and after sentences are by Helen Osborne, Health Literacy Consulting.

Here are some of the changes and why I made them:

- Began with an explanation of what antacids are.
- Defined "indigestion" in plain language by saying "feeling sick after you eat."
- Used a positive tone, starting with what people can do rather than what they cannot.

Strategies, Ideas, and Suggestions

Know and collaborate with your readers. From the first idea to review and publication, work with intended readers throughout the writing process. Know (generally, not specifically) about your reader's literacy level, language, age, culture, and interest in and familiarity with the subject matter.

Organization. Identify one primary message and support it with a limited number (usually three to five) of key points. I often choose these points by considering what readers should know, do, and feel as a result of reading this material.

Organize the key points in ways that make sense to readers (not just writers). Generally, this means starting with the concept of "what's in it for me" (WIIFM), which is a brief statement about why people should read this information. When writing a brochure about a new surgical procedure, for example, begin with how patients can benefit from this procedure rather than how many awards the medical facility has received for doing it. At the end of this brochure, summarize key points and include a list of resources for readers to learn more.

Obviously, when you write in plain language you can't include everything because documents would be too long. Instead, prioritize "need-to-know" skills and behaviors that readers must learn rather than "nice-to-know" background information that is not as essential. Make sure to also address topics that interest readers. Often these topics include practical considerations like costs and time.

Readability. Generally, plain language materials should be written at a sixth–eighth grade reading level. This level, however, is a guide and not a rigid rule. The best way to know if your material is understandable is to ask readers and not just rely on reading grade level formulas. (To learn more about assessing readability, go to Assessing Readability on page 13.)

Words. In truth, it is sometimes hard to choose the "just right" words—especially when writing about medical information that has a lot of technical terms. If possible, use common one- and two-syllable words that people already know and understand. An example is "heart attack" instead of "myocardial infarction."

But there certainly are times when you need a more difficult technical term. When this is the case, define the term, show how to pronounce it, and include a simply-worded example or explanation. For instance, "Bronchitis, bron-ki-tis, a disease that makes you cough."

Here are some other factors to consider when choosing words:

- Avoid "he/she" awkwardness by using plural pronouns like "they."

- Choose one term and use it consistently. For example, if you use "bandage," have it throughout the booklet rather than sometimes using "bandage" and other times "gauze" and "compress."

- Be sensitive to words that sound alike such as "gait" and "gate," or words that have more than one meaning such as "stool," "dressing," and "appendix."

(To learn more about words, go to Word Choice on page 257.)

Acronyms. An acronym is an artificial term made of initial letters from a group of words. Acronyms can be very difficult for people to understand because:

- Readers do not always know what the letters stand for. To make it clearer, explain the acronym in parentheses the first time it is used, as "Health Maintenance Organization (HMO)" or "HMO (Health Maintenance Organization)"

- Acronyms can have different meanings depending on the context. For example "AAA" can stand for the American Automobile Association, the Area Agency on Aging, or an Aortic Abdominal Aneurysm. Make sure readers know what your acronym means.

- Acronyms are not always pronounced as they look. For example, "HIPAA" (Health Insurance Portability and Accountability Act) is pronounced as a single word, while "CHF" (congestive heart failure) is pronounced as three distinct letters.

- Readers may be overwhelmed by too many acronyms. Try to minimize how many you use; choose only those that are

"CHF" (congestive heart failure) is pronounced as three distinct letters.

- Readers may be overwhelmed by too many acronyms. Try to minimize how many you use; choose only those that are for the readers' benefit, not yours. To make it easier for readers to understand, you might include a box with a summary of all the acronyms used.

Sentences. Plain language sentences should have just one main idea. Ideally, sentences will have no more than 15 words. This lessens the chance of having complex sentences with lots of commas and clauses. Often, you can use bullet points instead of overly long sentences.

Try to avoid conditional (if/then) sentences in which readers must make sense of two clauses and the relation between them. For example, instead of "If you think it might rain then bring an umbrella" write "It may rain so bring an umbrella."

Tone. Plain language documents should have a friendly and conversational tone, though not be overly chatty or cute. Tone should match the content—sad or difficult subjects should not be treated lightly. Here are some tips about tone:

- Write as though you were talking, using personal pronouns like "you" and "your." One way to achieve this tone is by reading aloud as you write and edit.

- Use an active, rather than passive, voice such as "your child will get a blood test," rather than "blood tests will be given to all children."

- Present information in as positive a manner as possible. This may be starting instructions with what patients can (rather than cannot) do. Positive information should also be

Layout and Design. How written materials look is as important as how they read. Here are ways to design documents that are inviting and appealing:

- Write in a font size that is large enough to see. Generally, this is 12-point type; 14- or 16-point type is preferable when writing for older readers or those who have limited vision. Avoid stylized or italic letters and instead use more traditional type such as Times New Roman or Arial.

- Use a combination of upper and lower case, rather than all capital letters. This way, readers get visual cues about the letters they are seeing.

- Justify (line up) words on the left, not centered or on the right. Centered text often results in uneven spacing between words that makes reading more difficult.

- Allow adequate white space (blank areas without print). Generally this is about a 50/50 split between print and white space. Have margins that are at least an inch wide. This is not only easy on the eyes but also allows room for people to add their own notes, comments, questions, or doodles.

- Have visual contrast between letters and background. This usually is black type on white or light, non-glossy paper. When you make copies, make sure that the print is clean and easy to see. Sometimes, copies of copies are almost unreadable.

- Use headers to identify main topics. Often, the most informative ones are written as questions such as "What is Diabetes?"

- Draw attention to key points by using bold and adding arrows or "call-out" boxes.

- Keep similar items together, and do not carry over just a sentence or two to the next page.

Graphics. Pictographs, illustrations, and photographs can aid understanding. Here are some tips to keep in mind:

- Generally, select graphics that are informative and not just decorative. Sometimes, however, decorative designs are so appealing that they motivate people to read. When this is the case, use the designs as long as they do not distract from the message.

- Use recognizable images rather than abstract symbols which might be misunderstood. For example, a red circle with a slash across it is commonly understood by people in the United States to mean "don't" but may not be as familiar to those from other parts of the world.

- Show and tell readers the correct way to perform tasks by having pictures with simple written captions beneath them. This can be very effective, for example, when showing each step in a sequence of instructions.

- Select pictures that are culturally relevant and appropriate to your audience, such as drawings of healthy, active seniors in a brochure for older adults.

- Draw internal body parts in context of the entire body. This not only conveys size and proportion, but also avoids "disembodied body parts" which people may find confusing or upsetting. To show detail, include an enlargement of the body part alongside the larger illustration.

(To learn more, go to Pictographs on page 175 and Visuals on page 245.)

Interaction. Have ways for readers to interact with written materials. You can do this, for example, with check-off boxes, fill-in-the blank exercises, or short quizzes. You can also have lines or spaces for patients to write their provider's name or next appointment time.

Feedback. Ask your intended readers to review drafts of your written material. Find out what they think about the document's organization, words, tone, layout, and graphics. Allow sufficient time not only to make their recommended changes but also to test the document again to make sure you didn't introduce new problems.

Plain language uses organization, words, sentences, tone, layout, graphics, and interaction to help make written materials more appealing and easier to read.

Sources to Learn More

AMC Cancer Research Center, 1994. *Beyond the Brochure: Alternative Approaches to Effective Health Communication.* Center for Disease Control and Prevention. Available at http://www.cdc.gov/cancer/nbccedp. Accessed January 24, 2004.

Centre for Literacy, Research Briefs on Health Communications, "Plain language and patient education: A summary of current research." Available at http://www.nald.ca/PROVINCE/QUE/litcent/health/briefs/no1/1.htm. Accessed May 16, 2004.

National Cancer Institute, 1994. *Clear & Simple: Developing Effective Print Materials for Low-Literate Readers.* National Institutes of Health.

National Literacy and Health Program, 1998. *Creating Plain Language Forms for Seniors: A Guide for the Public, Private, and Not-for-Profit Sectors.* Canadian Public Health Association. Available at http://www.nlhp.cpha.ca/publications.htm. Accessed January 20, 2004.

The Medical Library Association. *Deciphering medspeak.* Available at www.mlanet.org. Accessed January 26, 2004.

Doak CC, Doak LG, Root JH, 1996. *Teaching Patients with Low Literacy Skills,* 2nd ed. Philadelphia, PA: J.B. Lippincott Company.

Kimble J, 1995. *The Scribes Journal of Legal Writing: Answering the Critics of Plain Language.* Lansing, MI: Thomas Cooley Law School.

McGee J, 1999. *Writing and Designing Print Materials for Beneficiaries: A Guide for State Medicaid Agencies.* HCFA Publication Number 10145. Baltimore, MD: Centers for Medicare & Medicaid Services, U.S. Department of Health and Human Services. (A second edition is forthcoming in 2004. For ordering information, contact Jeanne McGee, McGee & Evers Consulting, Inc., Vancouver, Washington, 360-574-4744, jmcgee@pacifier.com).

National Institute for Literacy/ LINCS. (Large database of adult education and literacy resources, including LINCSearch, MyLINCS, and the Health & Literacy Special Collection/Compendium.) Web site: www.nifl.gov/lincs.

National Literacy and Health Program, 1998. *Easy Does It! Plain Language and Clear Verbal Communication.* Ontario, Canada: Canadian Public Health Association.

Osborne H, 2004. "In other words... adult learners and healthcare communication," *On Call* magazine, (3):16–17. Available at http://www.healthliteracy.com. Accessed May 15, 2004. Information is adapted and reprinted with permission of *On Call* magazine. *On Call* is published by BostonWorks, a division of the *Boston Globe.*

_____, 2000. *Overcoming Communication Barriers in Patient Education.* Gaithersburg, MD: Aspen Publishers, Inc. Information is adapted and reprinted with the author's permission.

_____, 1999. "In other words... getting through... lives can depend on simplifying the written word," *On Call* magazine, 2(9):42–43. Available at http://www.healthliteracy.com. Accessed January 24, 2004. Information is adapted and reprinted with permission of *On Call* magazine. *On Call* is published by BostonWorks, a division of the *Boston Globe.*

Scientific and Technical Information Simply Put, 1999. Atlanta, GA: Centers for Disease Control and Prevention.

PlainLanguage.gov. Available at http://www.plainlanguage.gov. Accessed January 26, 2004.

Plain Language Association International. Available at http://www.plainlanguagenetwork.org. Accessed January 26, 2004.

Schriver KA, 1997. *Dynamics in Document Design.* New York, NY: John Wiley & Sons, Inc.

Williams R, 1994. *The Non-Designers Design Book.* Berkeley, CA: Peachpit Press.

Quality

Starting Points

Quality healthcare is safe, effective, patient-centered, timely, efficient, and equitable. The Institute of Medicine defines quality as "providing patients with appropriate services in a technically competent manner with good communication, shared-decision making and cultural sensitivity"(IOM, 2001). The United States Agency for Healthcare Research and Quality defines quality healthcare simply as "doing the right thing, at the right time, for the right person, and having the best possible results" (AHRQ, 1998).

However you define quality healthcare, health literacy is an essential element. According to Linda Johnston Lloyd, who chairs the Health Literacy Work Group at the United States Health Resources and Services Administration, "health literacy promotes all quality goals by helping patients navigate the healthcare system, get needed information, and also ties in with patient safety." Lloyd sees health literacy as a flight of stairs, with the highest level being when patients make appropriate health decisions. Here is how she visualizes health literacy:

Figure 1.1. Promote Health Literacy. *From Health Resources and Services Administration, Health Literacy Presentation by Linda Johnston Lloyd, HRSA Center for Quality.*

Strategies, Ideas, and Suggestions

Provide quality information. Make sure that your health information is accurate, up-to-date, relevant, and communicated in ways your intended audience can understand. To accomplish this, find out what people need to know and are curious about. Find out in general about their culture, language, age, and literacy level. Then tailor your communication to meet individual needs. This may include choosing plain language written materials, demonstrating on models and objects, or leading community-based presentations. Also make sure to review your information on a regular basis—at least once a year, and even more often when there are new scientific findings or health recommendations.

Make sure your office is patient-centered. Verbally and nonverbally, welcome patients from the moment they first contact your office. Have staff who greet patients and help them feel comfortable and at ease. Create an environment in which patients can ask questions and raise concerns without fear of embarrassment. A patient-centered office is also easy for patients to get to and get around. Your office should not only be accessible to people with disabilities but also convey a sense of respect, caring, and good communication.

Go where patients are. Rather than only providing healthcare in traditional medical settings, consider also meeting with patients in the communities where they live and work. For instance, you might have community health workers and peer educators meet with people in their homes and community centers and teach health practices that are in keeping with people's languages, cultures, and traditions.

Confirm that patients understand. Use strategies like the "teach-back" technique to confirm that you and patients fully understand one another. This includes asking open-ended questions. For example, after you teach about proper nutrition you might ask, "When you make breakfast tomorrow, what will you eat (cook)?"

Sometimes providers are reluctant to confirm understanding, fearing that this process will take too long. In practice, however, confirming that patients do understand takes less time than dealing with problems that can occur when they do not. (To learn about the interactive communication loop, go to Talking and Listening on page 211.)

Make a personal commitment to quality. Admittedly, it is hard to make changes in how you communicate health information. One way to start is by making a personal commitment and asking yourself, "What can I do today to make a difference?" You might begin by focusing this week on just one aspect of "doing the right thing, at the right time, with the right person." Build on a series of small successes and, soon, quality health communication will be a routine part of your patient care.

Quality healthcare means, "doing the right thing, at the right time, for the right person, and having the best possible results."

Sources to Learn More

Agency for Healthcare Research and Quality, 1998. *Your Guide to Choosing Quality Health Care.* U.S. Department of Health and Human Services.

Health Resources and Services Administration, Health Literacy Work Group at http://www.hrsa.gov/quality/healthliteracy.htm. Accessed May 16, 2004.

Institute of Medicine, 2001. *Crossing the Quality Chasm: A New Health System for the 21st Century.* Washington, D.C.: National Academy Press.

Risk
Communication

Starting Points

Risk has to do with chance—most often, the chance that something will go wrong. The goal of most risk communication is to give people the information they need to make decisions and to take action. For example, public service campaigns can present the risks and benefits of flu shots. Risk is also discussed one-to-one in clinical settings, such as when physicians present treatment options like surgery or clinical trials and give patients information to make reasoned choices.

People perceive risk as much by feelings as by facts. This may be based on their sense of optimism, pessimism, or hope. Other risk perception factors include people's familiarity with the risk, whether or not they have any control over it, if the risk information is from trusted sources, and whether risks affect their children, themselves, or the public at large (Ropeik, Gray, 2002). Factor in, as well, any sensational news people might have heard about comparable risks.

To help people better understand risk information, use words, numbers, analogies, graphics, stories, and examples they relate to and can understand. Since they may be under stress and over-whelmed with too much information, allow sufficient time for people to absorb risk information, review alternatives, and make decisions they feel are well-reasoned and fair.

Strategies, Ideas, and Suggestions

Frame risk information. Risk information is seldom simple and straight-forward. Here are some ways you can help frame it:

- Be clear about timeframes and let people know whether this risk is an immediate concern or more likely to be problematic in a year, five years, or over a lifetime.

- Specify which risk you are talking about. Is it the risk of getting a disease, having a recurrence, or dying from it?

- Decide whether to talk about risk in positive or negative terms. In positive terms, you could say, "Studies show that 85% of people walk without pain after this type of surgery." In negative terms, this same risk could be stated as, "Fifteen percent of people who have this surgery still feel some pain when they walk."

- Consider whether to present risk in relative or absolute terms. Relative risk is a comparison, such as "Your are twice as likely to...." Absolute risk is a number, like "One out of four people will...."

- Keep in mind that many studies show that it is easier for people to understand risk when framed in positive and absolute terms.

Personalize information. Scientists and health providers are accustomed to thinking of risk in terms of populations, such as "27 out of 100 people feel dizzy after taking (x) medication." Patients and the general public, however, are usually much more concerned about their own vulnerability, "Will this medication make me dizzy?" To present risk data more personally, you could say, "While we don't know for sure how you will react, studies show that about 1 out of 4 people who take this medication get dizzy."

Word choice. Despite the care you take choosing the "just right" words to express risk, patients can easily overlook or misunderstand their exact meaning. For example, if you say that it is "probable" that surgery will be effective, a person may assume (partly based on hope) that this means that he or she will definitely get better. Shorthand words like these need to be clarified so patients can more clearly understand the risks they agree to take.

Numbers. Numbers, especially very big ones, are hard for most people to comprehend. Often, people will overestimate small risks and underestimate large ones. When communicating risk data, put it in terms people can relate to. For example, instead of saying, "483 people out of 1,000" you could more simply say "about 1 out of every 2 people." Don't over generalize, however, to the point that numbers are misleading. (To learn about numbers, go to Numbers on page 155).

Graphics. Numbers displayed in graphic formats such as tables, risk ladders, stick or facial displays, bar graphs, line graphs and pie charts can be quite helpful. Each of these graphic formats has benefits and drawbacks. Risk experts, however, have yet to agree on which are the most effective ones to use.

Metaphors and comparisons. You can also express risk through analogies or examples. Choose a comparison that the other person can relate to yet doesn't trivialize the risk. You can choose positive ones like the odds of winning the lottery or negative ones such as the chance of being injured in a car accident. Whatever example or metaphor you use, make it clear that this comparison is imprecise and only a way to begin thinking about risk.

Signs, Maps, and Other Navigation Tools

Starting Points

People often have difficulty finding their way around unfamiliar locations. Health facilities are no exception. When patients and visitors get lost, they may feel annoyed or embarrassed. They also might be late for appointments, resulting in costly scheduling snafus for providers.

Some way-finding problems relate to people. Patients and other visitors may have difficulty finding their way around health facilities because they are preoccupied or distracted, perhaps thinking more about their upcoming appointments than where they are going. Also, many people—especially those with limited literacy skills—have trouble reading complicated documents like maps (Kirsch, et al., 1993).

Other times directional problems are due to how signs, maps, and other navigation tools are designed or used. At times, these tools seem more helpful to employees who already know where they're going than to visitors arriving for the first time.

Most often, problems occur when there are mismatches between people and navigation tools. When lost and confused, many people (myself included) simply ask a "friendly face" to point them in the right direction.

"Nancy" has an appointment for a routine mammogram at a hospital where she hasn't been before. Her navigation troubles start as soon as she gets there, for she doesn't know whether to drive into the parking lot marked "Visitors" or "Patients." Since both lots are full, Nancy takes the only space she finds in an area farther away. When she gets to the hospital, Nancy is uncertain whether to go through the entrance marked "Ambulatory Care" or the one labeled "Visitor's Entrance." She assumes that "ambulatory" means the same as "out-patient" and therefore is the correct one to use. But her assumption is obviously incorrect as she finds a long corridor with mostly closed doors and no reception area. Now frustrated and already late for her appointment, Nancy asks someone for help. This person kindly tells her how to get to mammography which, to Nancy's amusement, has a sign saying "X-ray." Once there, she asks so everyone can hear, "Am I in the right place?"

Strategies, Ideas, and Suggestions

Exterior signs. Exterior (outside) signs should clearly identify which doors to enter. Wording should be familiar and easy to understand by all visitors, including those with limited literacy or language skills. Problems arise with jargon like "Ambulatory Entrance" which, some visitors might assume, is for ambulances and not patients.

Interior signs. Interior (inside) signs also need to be clear. Many times, signs have several tiers of information like a newspaper's headline, subhead, and text. The name of the benefactor who donated money may be at the top, as in "The Jones Center." Next might be the official department name or service, such as "Radiology." It's only at the bottom of the sign that visitors find the term they are looking for, like "Mammography" or "X-ray."

The Jones Center Radiology Department X-ray and Mammography	**X-Ray and Mammography** Radiology Department The Jones Center

You want to find the X-Ray Department. Which sign do you find more helpful?

Figure 1.1. Sample Signs

To make interior signs easier to understand, reverse the order and have the most commonly-used term in big lettering at the top. This helps people know where to go and reassures them once they get there.

Consistent terms. Whether in signs, maps, or when talking, use consistent wording. For example, decide whether visitors can purchase snacks in the "Café," "Cafeteria," or "Dining Room."

Signs in other languages and in Braille. Make sure that your signs are useful to all visitors, including those who do not speak English or cannot see. Translate important signs into the most common languages used by your patient population. As well, have signs in Braille and raised lettering for those who are visually impaired.

Visuals. Signs sometimes have visuals in addition to, or instead of, words. These include universally recognized symbols like wheelchairs meaning "handicapped accessible." In addition to being understandable, visuals and symbols should also convey respect. This means not stereotyping or stigmatizing a group such as signs of the elderly shown only as stooped-over people with canes.

Facilities might also create their own signs which may be clever and attractive, but are not always clear. More than once, I've been confused by visuals indicating which restroom to use. As with printed information, clarify by adding a simply written word or phrase beneath each visual. And then test the sign with intended readers to make sure your message is correctly understood.

Place signs uniformly. Place signs where visitors naturally look for them. And be consistent so that people don't have to constantly shift their focus from walls to ceilings, floors, doorways, and windows.

Maps. Maps are hard for many people to read and use. In addition to literacy difficulties, people may be unable to see the teeny, tiny type used on many maps. As well, some maps are out-of-date and do not include the latest changes of where departments are now located.

Other navigation tools. In addition to signs and maps, some facilities use navigation tools like color-coded lines or symbols (such as shoe prints) embedded in the floor. When you use colors to distinguish spaces, have additional ways for people who are colorblind or visually impaired to find their way. Make sure, as well, to update your navigation tools to be consistent with where departments now are. One easy way to do this is with arrows that are moved when necessary.

Asking directions. Asking directions is easy for some people, but very difficult or embarrassing for others. For example, a man with dyslexia didn't want to let anyone know that he couldn't read. When he found "exit" rather than "X-ray," he simply walked out the door. You can make it easier for all visitors by offering help in a friendly and supportive way, such as by asking, "How can I help? What department are you looking for?"

Giving directions. Facilities often have Information Desks in their lobbies with staff or volunteers who give directions. While very helpful, these desks are not necessarily where visitors get lost. Sometimes people will ask for help from anyone who looks like he or she might know the area.

Teach all employees (service workers as well as clinical and administrative staff) how to give directions. This includes not only telling visitors where to turn left or right but also landmarks to look for along the way. By saying "turn left at the water fountain," visitors don't have to guess whether that turn is a hallway or just an alcove. Even better than just giving directions is encouraging staff to take the time to walk people to their destinations. In all instances, employees should acknowledge when they don't know directions and find someone who can better help lost visitors.

Take a tour. One of the best ways to find out how well your signs, maps, and other navigation tools work is by accompanying a visitor (perhaps a family member or friend) as he or she navigates through your facility the first time. Let this person lead the way and help refresh your memory about what it is like to be a newcomer. Then, of course, make all the needed navigational changes.

One of the best ways to find out how well your signs, maps, and other navigation tools work is by accompanying a visitor (perhaps a family member or friend) as he or she navigates through your facility the first time.

Sources to Learn More

Centre for Literacy of Quebec, 2001. *Health Literacy Project, Phase 1: Needs Assessment of the Health Education and Information Needs of Hard-to-Reach Patients.* Available at http://www.nald.ca/litcent.htm. Accessed January 23, 2004.

Gale RP, et al, 2003. "Depiction of elderly and disabled people on road traffic signs: International comparison," *BMJ*, 327:1456–1457.

Harvard School of Public Health: Health Literacy Studies website. Available at http://www.hsph.harvard.edu/healthliteracy/links.html. Accessed May 18, 2004.

Kirsch I, Jungeblut A, Jenkins L, Kolstad A, 1993. *Adult Literacy in America.* Washington, D.C.: National Center for Education Statistics.

Osborne H, 2001. "In other words...tools to help patients navigate their way around hospitals," *On Call* magazine, 4(10):26–27. Available at http://www.healthliteracy.com. Accessed January 22, 2004. Information is adapted and reprinted with permission of *On Call* magazine. *On Call* is published by BostonWorks, a division of the *Boston Globe*.

Stories and Narratives

Starting Points

Stories (and their close "cousin," narratives) are powerful health communication tools. Combining emotions and facts, stories help people connect with health information in a very personal way. Audiences of all ages and cultures relate to stories because they help people bridge differences and find qualities they have in common. Stories are not only engaging and entertaining, but also easy for most everyone to understand—even by those who have trouble reading or paying attention.

Distinct from other types of communication, stories have a beginning, middle, and end, though not always in that order. They also have characters (real or imagined) who convey feelings and communicate ideas.

Stories are told by storytellers to an audience of one or many. In healthcare, this is likely to happen in one of four ways:

- *Health providers tell stories to patients.* Providers may use stories to raise awareness about general health or wellness issues, or to focus more specifically on an illness and its treatment. An example is a story about how Henrietta works at a computer all day but has fewer neck aches now that she regularly goes to a fitness center.

- *Patients tell stories to health providers.* Perhaps prompted by their providers, patients can tell stories about what it's like to live with a particular disease or condition. Providers should listen carefully to what patients do and do not say. By listening, providers are likely to hear about the patient's physical, psychological, and emotional state, all woven together.

- *Health professionals tell stories to health professionals.* Whether called case studies, vignettes, or scenarios, stories not only include facts and figures but also values. This can be of great benefit, especially when talking to colleagues of different disciplines or points of view. A cardiologist, for example, might share a story about a patient who has bypass surgery, while a holistic medicine practitioner might talk about a patient with a similar diagnosis who uses herbal remedies.

- *Patients tell stories to patients.* When people hear a story being told, they connect with the teller in a personal way—getting the sense that the teller is "just like me." This happens regardless of whether the storyteller is famous (perhaps an actor or political figure) or anonymous (like a member of a self-help group).

—From Kevin Brooks, PhD, storyteller/researcher

Strategies, Ideas, and Suggestions

Telling stories. When telling stories in healthcare settings, make sure the stories have a point and are not simply entertaining. Sometimes, you will need to highlight what the point is, perhaps by saying "Let me tell you about a person who…" Other times, the point is more evident. Stories don't always have to be spoken. Indeed, like in this book, stories are sprinkled throughout to clarify key points and make them "come alive."

Encouraging patients to tell stories. By listening to stories, providers can learn a lot about their patients' strengths, concerns, and points of view. You can encourage patients to tell you stories by saying "Tell me about a time that…" or "Give me an example of the problems you have when. …"

Stories needn't take a lot of time. If you feel that patients are talking in too roundabout a way, help them focus by saying something like "You started talking about your heart and now you're telling me about your feet. Please tell me more about how these problems connect." Being directive like this is preferable to asking patients to be "brief" which may cause them to filter out details that may or may not be important.

Listening. When listening to stories—especially ones told by patients—consider the story in its entirety. If the story doesn't make sense, find out what is missing or what is wrong. Encourage patients to listen to their own stories, as well. It's likely that the version they tell you differs in some way from the one they share with family and friends. Make sure you understand patients' stories correctly, perhaps by saying, "Let me tell you what I've heard" or "Correct me if I have any of the details wrong." And, of course, thank patients for sharing their stories.

Heroes and resistance. Stories generally have several characters, at least one being a hero who overcomes obstacles or meets with resistance. Often, the hero shares qualities similar to those of the teller. Resistance is apt to be from characters with different beliefs, values, and experiences. Depending on who is telling the story, these characters may differ in important ways. For example, a provider may characterize resistance as patients who don't follow treatment plans. Patients, instead, may frame the same factors as just facts of life.

Truth, facts, and fiction. Stories need not stand alone. Especially in healthcare settings, presentations need to also include data, numbers, and other "hard facts." Sometimes stories and facts are presented as one, as in children's stories that have a wise character introducing health information. Other times, they are presented in tandem, such as in a keynote speech that has both research data and case stories.

Regardless of their structure, stories should always be true—though not necessarily all factual. It is the storyteller's responsibility to craft stories in ways that help the audience relate to and make sense of essential truths.

Talking about stories. Rather than a one-way conversation in which a speaker talks at an audience, stories encourage thought and discussion. When presenting to a community group, for example, you might preface a story by saying, "Here's what happened to someone I know" rather than "Here's how to do it." After the story, you can invite audience participation by asking, "Have you ever experienced anything like that?" or "If you were the person in the story, what would you do differently?"

Set the stage for discussion by knowing ahead of time a little about your audience, including their age, culture, and familiarity with the subject matter. Throughout the story, notice peoples' responses, facial expressions, and body movements. And then adapt your presentation to meet the ever-changing needs of your story-telling audience.

Combining emotion and facts, stories help people connect with health information in a very personal way.

Sources to Learn More

National Storytelling Network. Available at http://www.storynet.org. Accessed January 27, 2004.

Newman TB, 2003. "The power of stories over statistics," *BMJ*, 327:1424–1427.

Osborne H, 2002. "In other words...narrative power...using stories in health-care communication," *On Call* magazine, 5(5):30–31. Available at http://www.healthliteracy.com. Accessed January 22, 2004. Information is adapted and reprinted with permission of *On Call* magazine. *On Call* is published by BostonWorks, a division of the *Boston Globe*.

Talking and Listening

Starting Points

Talking and listening is the most common form of health communication. But just because this type of communication happens a lot doesn't mean it is always easy. In fact, talking and listening can be quite difficult. In part, this is because providers often talk about complicated concepts (like risks and benefits), abstract ideas (such as wellness and health promotion), and use multi-syllabic words and medical jargon that may sound to patients like a foreign language. As well, patients may have trouble listening or concentrating when they are stunned by bad news, scared, sick, or in pain.

Despite these challenges, providers have a responsibility to communicate health information in ways that patients and their families or caregivers can understand. Patients must be able to understand their diagnoses, participate in treatment decisions, consent (or not) to procedures, follow self-care instructions, and recognize and take appropriate action in medical emergencies.

Talking and listening don't always happen one-to-one or face-to-face between a single provider and patient. Today, many health conversations also include family members, caregivers, interpreters, and medical specialists. And patient-provider conversations are not necessarily in-person, but can take place over the phone or by computer.

Regardless of where or how you meet, it is your responsibility as a health provider to confirm that everyone in the conversation understands. One way to do this is through the "Interactive Communication Loop," a technique outlined by Dean Schillinger, MD and associates.

The interactive communication loop involves:

- Introducing a new concept about a patient's health or condition

- Following up with an assessment of the patient's recall and comprehension

- Clarifying or tailoring the message if the patient does not understand

- Reassessing the patient's recall and comprehension

- Continuing this loop until a common understanding has been achieved (Schillinger, et al., 2003)

Strategies, Ideas, and Suggestions

Rapport. Set a positive tone by beginning conversations with a smile and warm handshake. Introduce yourself by the name you wish to be called and, in turn, ask patients how they prefer to be addressed. Meet patients at eye level; sit down if they are seated or in bed. Often, you can build rapport by first chatting about non-medical matters such as the weather or current events. Make sure the person you are talking with is not so distracted or uncomfortable that meaningful conversation is impossible.

Shame-free environment. Create an environment in which patients can comfortably say when they do and do not understand. When they admit confusion or look perplexed, let patients know that many people have trouble learning health information. Appreciate, too, that patients may forget what you say, especially after they hear bad news. And when patients try to make necessary lifestyle changes—even if they're not successful—acknowledge attempts and compliment them for trying.

Physical space. The space you meet in is almost as important as the topics you discuss. Try to find a private, quiet, well-lit place in which to talk. If a separate room is not available, at least pull curtains or move chairs to create a sense of privacy. And sit near each other to minimize physical barriers such as bed rails and desks.

Agenda. At the start of each meeting, decide with patients how best to use the time. Ask patients what they hope to accomplish and together agree on topics to address now or save for another time. Once you know the agenda, talk about topics in a logical order. Of course, there are apt to be many "branch points" when you and patients must decide where to go next in the conversation.

Listening. Listening—really hearing what others have to say—is hard for almost everyone. Give patients your undivided attention and make sure you fully understand their perspectives and concerns. You can do this by encouraging patients to fully state their thoughts by saying "that's interesting," or "please tell me more." Make sure not to interrupt and, instead, make a note to yourself of issues to revisit when the patient stops talking.

Make sure you not only listen but also understand. Periodically stop and repeat back what you hear patients say. This way you not only confirm that you "get it" but also demonstrate that you are listening and paying attention.

Make sure you not only listen but also understand. Periodically stop and repeat back what you hear patients say. This way you not only confirm that you "get it" but also demonstrate that you are listening and paying attention.

Learning and teaching. Education is at the core of most health conversations. Ideally, this means mutual learning with providers talking about medical information and patients sharing what it is like to live with their illnesses or conditions. Begin by finding out what patients already know and then adding new information as they are ready to learn.

Be as clear, specific, and concrete as possible and put new information into context. For example, you could say something like, "This new exercise is like the one you have been doing, except you now need to...." After introducing new information, allow sufficient time for patients to process, reflect, and ask questions.

Words. Healthcare has its own vocabulary. For example, medical jargon like "dressing" has nothing to do with clothing, salads, or turkeys. Terms like "formulary" and acronyms (new "words" made up from longer phrases) such as "ADL" and "HIPAA" may be unknown to patients. Patients can get understandably confused when health professionals interchange words like "hypertension" and "high blood pressure."

To communicate more understandably, choose your words carefully. When you truly need a word that patients don't already know, explain it and give an example. For instance, say "ADLs—Activities of Daily Living, like getting dressed or eating." Often, you can take cues from patients about which words to use. For example, if they say "sugar" rather than "diabetes," you should feel comfortable doing the same. (To learn more about words, go to Word Choice on page 257.)

they continually interrupt. When meeting with several people, such as a patient and two family members, suggest that the patient sit slightly in front of the others. This way, you not only can focus your attention on the patient but also see the family member's reactions.

Learning styles and needs. Be sensitive to peoples' communication styles and needs, especially in regard to literacy, language, and physical or cognitive abilities. For example, when talking with someone who has limited literacy skills or trouble concentrating, present information in small "bite-sized pieces" rather than larger "chunks." This gives the person an easier way to learn, reflect, and remember.

When talking with a person from another language or culture, ask if a trained interpreter would be helpful. And when communicating with a person who is hard of hearing, face the person directly and make sure to not cover your mouth or chew gum. However, it's neither necessary nor helpful to shout or over-enunciate words. (To learn more about communicating with people who are Deaf or hard of hearing, go to Hearing: Communicating with People Who Are Deaf or Hard of Hearing on page 79.)

Distractions and interruptions. Many factors can interfere with or disrupt spoken communication. While you can't control them all, do what you can to minimize distractions. Meet in a private space (or at least one that feels private) that is not within earshot of overhead pages or a lot of foot traffic. As well, clean off the clutter on your desk or in your office to reduce visual distractions. And, if possible, put your beeper on vibrate and turn off the phone ringer. It certainly interrupts the flow of conversation when patients hear their providers say, "I'll be there in a minute—I'm just finishing up with this patient."

Other ways of communicating. Reinforce verbal information with other forms of communication. Provide written materials for patients to read and share with others. You can also create drawings that illustrate key points, or use metaphors and stories that make abstract concepts more real. As well, make it easy for patients to learn as much as they want to know by telling them about books, tapes, websites, hotlines, consumer health libraries, local support groups, national associations, and other resources where they can find more information.

Confirming understanding. Make sure that you and patients truly understand each other. Start by putting responsibility on yourself (where it rightfully belongs) by saying something along the lines of, "Let me see if I've made myself clear." Then ask relevant and specific open-ended questions like, "Some parents wonder when to call our office. If your child's fever goes over 102 degrees, what will you do?" Or, "What will you tell your friends about this illness?" And, after talking about the dosage for a new liquid medication, you might say, "Show me which sized spoon you will use to take this medicine."

Sometimes, despite your best efforts to communicate clearly, patients still do not understand. If this is the case, then consider whether there are other factors like learning disabilities, communication disorders such as hearing loss, cognitive impairments, depression, limited literacy or language skills, or cultural differences that get in the way of talking, listening, and understanding.

Providers often talk about complicated concepts (like risks and benefits), abstract ideas (such as wellness and health promotion), and use multi-syllabic words and medical jargon that may sound like a foreign language to patients.

Sources to Learn More

American Academy on Physician and Patient. Available at http://www.physicianpatient.org. Accessed January 27, 2004.

Gordon GH, 2002. "Care not cure: Dialogues at the transition," *Journal of Clinical Outcomes Management*, 9(12):677–681.

Kessels RPC, 2003. "Patients' memory for medical information," *Journal of the Royal Society of Medicine*, 96:219–222.

Lipkin M, Lazare A, Putnam SM, 1995. *The Medical Interview*. New York, NY:Springer Verlag.

Maguire P, Pitceathly C, 2002. "Key communication skills and how to acquire them," *BMJ*, 325:697–700.

National Literacy and Health Program, 1998. *Easy Does It! Plain Language and Clear Verbal Communication*. Ontario, Canada: Canadian Public Health Association.

Osborne H, 2003a. Communicating with clients in person and over the phone, *Issues Brief*, Center for Medicare Education, 4(8). Available at http://www.medicareed.org.

_____, 2003b. "In other words…opening the interactive communication loop," *On Call* magazine, 6(5):16–17. Available at http://www.healthliteracy.com. Accessed January 27, 2004. Information is adapted and reprinted with permission of *On Call* magazine. *On Call* is published by BostonWorks, a division of the *Boston Globe*.

_____, 2002. *Partnering with Patients To Improve Health Outcomes*. Gaithersburg, MD: Aspen Publishers, Inc. Information is adapted and reprinted with the author's permission.

_____, 2001. "In other words…know when to speak and when to listen…communicating with people who are anxious or angry," *On Call* magazine, 4(8):34–35. Available at http://www.healthliteracy.com. Accessed January 27, 2004. Information is adapted and reprinted with permission of *On Call* magazine. *On Call* is published by BostonWorks, a division of the *Boston Globe*.

_____, 2000. *Overcoming Communication Barriers in Patient Education*. Gaithersburg, MD: Aspen Publishers, Inc. Information is adapted and reprinted with the author's permission.

_____, 1999. "In other words…finding out what you need to know…the importance of better interviewing skills," *On Call* magazine. 2(12):42–43. Available at http://www.healthliteracy.com. Accessed January 27, 2004. Information is adapted and reprinted with permission of *On Call* magazine. *On Call* is published by BostonWorks, a division of the *Boston Globe*.

Schillinger D, Piette J, Grumbach K et al, 2003. "Closing the loop: Physician communication with diabetic patients who have low health literacy," *Archives of Internal Medicine*, 163:83–90.

Schultz M, 2002. "Low literacy skills needn't hinder care," *RN*. April.

White JC, et al, 1997. "Wrapping things up: A qualitative analysis of the closing moments of the medial visit," *Patient Education and Counseling*, 30:155–165.

Talking and Listening

Telephone

Starting Points

In today's busy and wired world, a lot of health communication takes place over the telephone. This communication includes: one-to-one conversations between patients and providers; conference calls with interpreters, families, or specialists far away; health information services that provide education and resources; "hotlines" and other crisis services; telephone triage and call centers where health professionals assess a patient's need for services; and recorded messages that you leave for others or they leave for you.

The telephone is a convenient way for patients and providers to stay in contact. It helps patients who cannot easily travel to see their providers. Additionally, patients and providers alike almost always save time when talking on the phone rather than meeting in person. But the telephone also has drawbacks. There are no visual cues to make a diagnosis or to confirm understanding. And a drawback to some is that the telephone is more impersonal and anonymous. To others, this is an advantage.

It's amazing how much information people reveal over the telephone. I marvel at how connections get made, like people's ability to show openness and provide information they hadn't talked about before. As a nurse, I know that the anonymity of a telephone conversation can sometimes reveal more than when people meet face to face.

—Julie Hodorowski, information services manager at the National Cancer Institute's Cancer Information Service of New York

Strategies, Ideas, and Suggestions

Have help in your voice. Help the person at the other end of the conversation absorb information by setting a pleasant tone. Be as positive as possible, saying "I will" and "I can," rather than "I won't" and "I can't." When you must say "no," state why and offer alternatives.

When the caller is cheerful or friendly, respond in a similar fashion. If the other person is sad or disappointed, be empathetic and acknowledge these feelings. And when the caller is angry or agitated, stay calm and try to soothe the situation.

Take responsibility for the direction of the conversation. Redirect talkative callers. For example, you can say, "I hear your concern about...I'd like to help and wonder if you called for an appointment."

Choose your words carefully. Since the phone is auditory only, make sure your words are easy for others to understand. As a rule, this means using common one- and two-syllable words, like saying "doctor" instead of "physician." It also means defining new or complicated terms, such as "durable medical equipment."

Choosing words carefully also entails explaining necessary acronyms (which are "new" words made up from a series of letters). For example, you could say, "CHF, which is short for congestive heart failure." (To learn more about words, go to Word Choice on page 256.)

Conference calls. Set ground rules and clear expectations for conference calls. Begin by designating a leader who is responsible for the call. The leader should give rules such as to identify yourself each time you speak, and put the call on mute if you're in a noisy environment. Then the leader should invite all participants to briefly introduce themselves. Throughout the call, the leader should make sure that everyone who wants to speak has the opportunity to do so. At the end of the call, the leader should summarize key points, ask for questions and clarification, and conclude by talking about next steps.

Distractions. People are often distracted when they are on the phone. Perhaps the person you are talking with has small children who want attention, or maybe a co-worker is knocking impatiently on your office door. Let the other person know if you are distracted. In turn, ask if you think the other person is not giving you his or her full attention.

Recording messages. When you leave a message on someone else's machine, speak slowly and clearly. Give your name and phone number at the beginning and again at the end; this way the other person hears twice how to reach you. It is also helpful to leave best times to return your call so as to avoid needless rounds of "telephone tag." Another tip is to stand up when recording voice messages. I've learned from experience that you're likely to sound much more energetic this way.

Phone trees. Telephone services often have phone trees with several options. To access these options you usually have prompts such

Telephone

as "press 1 to make an appointment, 2 to renew your prescription, or press 0 to speak with the operator." For many callers, these prompts are annoying and difficult to follow. Make it easier for callers by having only three or four prompts, including one to talk with a "real" person.

In our multi-lingual society, many organizations choose to have recorded messages and prompts in more than one language. Appreciate, however, that by doing so callers need to stay on the phone at least twice as long before they can get the information they want and need.

Communicating with people who are deaf or hard of hearing. A person who is deaf or hard of hearing may "talk" with you via a TTY (telephone-typewriter). While you use a standard telephone, he or she types into a small computer device that has a keyboard, screen, and modem. A phone relay operator facilitates communication by typing to the other person using the TTY and talking with you by phone. This service is offered at no charge through the telephone company. Look in your phone book for a local contact number.

Confirm understanding. In one-to-one conversations as well as on conference calls, stop periodically and confirm that all parties understand one another. Near the end of the call, summarize what you talked about and the actions everyone agrees to take. After the call, you may want to send a letter or brochure with additional resources and ways for people to learn more.

Beyond just talking. With the rapid advances in technology, the telephone may soon be used for more than just talking. For example, people can be connected by video phones which adds the benefit of seeing one another. And some medical tests, like electrocardiograms and blood pressure, can now be done with home-based electronic devices that communicate test results to the provider's office by phone.

The anonymity of a telephone conversation can sometimes reveal more than when people meet face to face.

Sources to Learn More

Car J, Sheikh A, 2003. "Telephone consultations," *BMJ*, 326:966–969.

Incoming Calls Management Institute. Available at http://www.incoming.com. Accessed January 27, 2004.

Ledlow GR, O'Hair HD, Moore S, 2003. "Predictors of communication quality: The patient, provider, and nurse call center triad," *Health Communication*, 15(4):431–455.

National Cancer Institute's (NCI's) Cancer Information Service of New York at 1–800-4-CANCER or online at http://www.cancer.gov. Accessed February 21, 2004.

Osborne H, 2003. Communicating with clients in person and over the phone, *Issues Brief*, Center for Medicare Education, 4(8). Available at http://www.medicareed.org. Accessed January 27, 2004.

———, 2000a. *Overcoming Communication Barriers in Patient Education.* Gaithersburg, MD: Aspen Publishers, Inc. Information is adapted and reprinted with the author's permission.

———, 2000b. "In other words…don't just stand there, answer," *On Call* magazine, 3(3):38–39. Available at http://www.healthliteracy.com. Accessed January 27, 2004. Information is adapted and reprinted with permission of *On Call* magazine. *On Call* is published by Boston Works, a division of the *Boston Globe*.

Telephone

Touchscreen Technology

Starting Points

Health information can now be communicated through touchscreen technology—a type of computer-based communication that uses audio, video, and interaction simultaneously. Similar to a bank's ATM machine, a touchscreen has no keyboard or mouse and is therefore easy for most people to use. People of all ages can learn at their own pace without feeling pressured or overwhelmed by too much information. Those who are inexperienced or uncomfortable with computers, have physical or cognitive disabilities, or limited literacy and language skills can all use touchscreens with great success.

Touchscreen technology is an efficient and effective way to teach. Modules can be designed to present basic health information in an organized and complete fashion. Clinical information can be updated to reflect changes in current practice. As well, new languages can be added fairly easily, assuming interpreters are available to do the narration. And learning feels personal and private—just between the patient and computer.

With touchscreen technology, patients get immediate feedback and reinforcement that learning has occurred. Also, providers can assess and document learning by asking patients to respond to a series of questions. These questions can be multiple choice (with several options including "not sure"), true/false, matching, or Likert scales ("choose a number from 1 to 5, with 1 being...and 5 being..."). The patients' answers are then printed out for patients and providers to review together.

The Cambridge Health Alliance in Cambridge, MA is using touchscreen technology at clinics throughout its organization. In the Tuberculosis (TB) Clinic, for example, new patients use a module (teaching program) that explains what TB is and introduces patients to the doctors and nurses they are about to meet. Both the text and the audio are available in several languages. Throughout the module, patients are asked to respond to multiple-choice questions by touching colored buttons that appear on the screen. Providers get a printout of each patient's response to this "quiz" and use it to identify areas that need reinforcement and clarification. Providers find that this information, plus their mandated clinical teaching, is an excellent place to start patient discussions.

Patients and providers alike are enthusiastic about touchscreen technology. Patients say they feel welcomed, relaxed, and better prepared to ask questions. As a bonus, some people are delighted with their newly found "computer" skills. Providers, too, acknowledge the benefits of touchscreen technology. They report that patients are better prepared for appointments because they already know a little about the disease and its treatment. This helps free up their time to focus on each patient's specific concerns. As the developers of this module agree, touchscreen technology doesn't replace clinical teaching—it just makes it more efficient and effective.

—From Tania Phocas and Yadira Ramos of the Department of Community Affairs at Cambridge Health Alliance in Cambridge, MA

Strategies, Ideas, and Suggestions

Housing and display. Since people only need access to the computer screen, touchscreens can be housed in kiosks (either stationary or on wheels) that protect the computer against theft and misuse. These kiosks can be in public places such as waiting rooms or in more private areas such as exam rooms. Partitions can be put up around the kiosks for added privacy and earphones can be added so the audio portion is not overheard. Patients who are in bed may use laptop computers instead.

Written information. Text should be easy-to-read and written at a level patients can understand. Use the principles of plain language, have common words people already know, explain new terms they need to learn, and display information in ways that look inviting and appealing to read.

It's also important to organize information from the patient's perspective. In the TB module, for example, one of the first things that patients learn on the touchscreen is that they probably do not have active TB disease. This concept is prominently placed because providers report that this is generally the first topic that patients want to know about.

Visual information. Whether you use simple line drawings, photographs, or both, make sure your visuals enhance (rather than distract from) the content. You not only can insert pictures of the actual providers who patients will be meeting with, but also can include culturally relevant visuals. For example, if the target population for your module on nutrition is Haitian, your visuals can include foods like rice, beans, and chicken that are part of their traditional diet.

Content. Develop modules with clinicians so that the educational content is identical to what is taught in practice. Use the same

Touchscreen Technology

words, examples, procedures, and equipment in the module as in the clinical setting.

In addition, modules can be used to assess readiness to change behavior. For example, you could find out where patients who smoke cigarettes are along the lines of the "Stages of Change" model (Prochaska, Norcross, DiClemente, 1994). Responses might include these four choices: "Are you planning to stop smoking in the next six months?"; "Are you planning to stop smoking in the next month?"; "Have you stopped smoking in the last six months?"; or "Have you stopped smoking for more than six months?"

Interaction. Touchscreens allow for ongoing assessment of patient understanding. You can ask several questions after each major topic area and again at the end. For example, after teaching how TB is contracted, you could ask "How do people get TB?" Then offer four choices: "Touching and kissing," "Sharing food with my family," "Breathing the same air as someone with active TB" and "I'm not sure how TB is spread." The program then tells patients whether their answer is correct or incorrect, and always reinforces the correct response.

Other languages. As long as interpreters and translators are available (whether in-house or through an outside service), the audio and text of each module can be in all the languages your patients use. Sometimes, you might even want two versions of the same language such as one in Portuguese for people from Brazil and another for people from Portugal.

Touchscreen technology takes a team. It takes a team to develop and update touchscreen modules. At a minimum, this team should include: administrators and clinicians to identify need, authorize budget, and select the most useful and feasible placement of each module; health educators or patient education experts to draft and review content; a technical developer who is proficient with technology; end users (patients) willing to test new modules; and a coordinator to oversee all aspects of module development and evaluation.

Technology skills required. Admittedly, a person needs advanced technical skills to create touchscreen modules. This person must not only be proficient with the required software and hardware, but also have the ability and willingness to make needed changes. "Information only" modules require less technical skill than those that are more interactive. Likewise, modules that always proceed in the same sequence are simpler to design than ones with automatically programmed skip questions such as "If yes, go to question 6."

Evaluation. Throughout the development process, test each module with end users. To make sure the module accomplishes what you hope it will, ask at least five people about:

- *Content.* Do people understand the key points? Can they identify the main ideas to be learned?

- *Narration.* Is the audio component too fast or too slow? Can the user understand the narrator's accent?

- *Visuals.* Do the users understand, like, and relate to the drawings or photographs? If visuals are instructional, can the user "teach back" the instructions?

- *Text.* Is the module written in ways people can read and understand? Are there any terms that need to be defined?

- *Interaction.* Is the module easy to use? What could make it more user-friendly?

Touchscreen technology doesn't replace clinical teaching—it just makes it more efficient and effective.

Sources to Learn More

Cambridge Health Alliance. Available at http://www.challiance.org. Accessed January 28, 2004.

Lewis D, 1999. "Computer-based approaches to patient education: A review of the literature," *Journal of the American Medical Informatics Association,* 6(4):272–282.

Neafsey PJ, Strickler Z, Shellman J, Padula AT, 2001. "Delivering health information about self-medication to older adults," *Journal of Gerontological Nursing,* November:19–27.

Osborne H, 2004. "In other words…teaching with touchscreen technology," *On Call* magazine, 7(1):16–17. Available at http://www.healthliteracy.com. Accessed January 27, 2004. Information is adapted and reprinted with permission of *On Call* magazine. *On Call* is published by Boston Works, a division of the *Boston Globe.*

Prochaska JO, Norcross JC, DiClemente CC, 1994. *Changing for Good: A Revolutionary Six-Stage Program for Overcoming Bad Habits and Moving Your Life Positively Forward.* New York, NY: Avon Books.

Wofford JL, Currin D, Michielutte R, Wofford MM, 2001. "The multimedia computer for low-literacy patient education: A pilot project of cancer risk perceptions," *Medscape General Medicine,* 3(2).

Translations

Starting Points

"Translation" refers to the process of converting written information from one language to another as opposed to "interpretation" which does the same with the spoken word. Translations help bridge communication between people who do not share a common language. Given that almost 46 million people in the United States speak a language other than English in their homes (U.S. Census, 2000), translations are increasingly important today.

Translations are very important in healthcare because so much information is communicated in writing. This includes discharge instructions, patient's rights, informed consent documents, medical bills, and even signs or maps that help newcomers find their way around unfamiliar places.

Patients have a basic right and need to understand measures taken on their behalf regardless of what type or level of language they speak. Effective communication via interpretation, translation, or other language aids can be a matter of life or death when the medical staff and patient don't speak the same language.

—From Russell K. Dollinger, PhD, publisher of *Pocket Medical Books*

Strategies, Ideas, and Suggestions

Translate documents. Work with professional translators whenever possible. Native translators, even more than those who are just bilingual, are especially likely to accurately capture all cultural nuances.

Keep in mind that professional translators are not necessarily health experts; that job belongs to you. To preserve the essence of your translated message, simplify it first in English. Rather than insist on a literal (word-for-word) translation, let the translator make needed adaptations for linguistic and cultural differences. Confirm that the translated document is accurate by asking a second person to translate it back into English (a "back translation"). Make sure that the typist or proofreader is also familiar with the language being used. Even well-translated documents can lose their meaning when important accent marks are omitted or misplaced.

Develop and test materials with intended readers. Translated information, just like all other types of communication, must be presented in ways people can understand and accept. To accomplish this, work with your intended readers throughout the translation process. Develop ideas, make decisions about word choice and illustrations, and test the final draft with your readers.

Inform patients about translations. I've seen many healthcare documents with statements at the bottom saying something like, "Please let us know if you need this booklet in (x) language." Ironically, these statements are only in English! Let patients know you can communicate with them by translating statements like these into their languages.

Two languages in one document. Sometimes healthcare organizations want two or more languages in the same document. These languages may be on the top and bottom of the same page or upside-down from each other. While these layouts can work well, they also present design challenges. For example, English is a

Translations

tighter language than most. This means it takes up less space than a language like Spanish which is about 20–30% larger. As a result, the text may look crowded when the two languages are together.

Examples and illustrations. Translated documents usually include more than just words. Make sure that the examples and illustrations you use are consistent with the culture, age, and interests of your readers. For example, when translating a nutrition brochure you might chose whether to mention tacos, egg rolls, crepes, or blintzes.

Word lists. Most languages have more than one way to describe an item, action, or idea. In English, for example, carbonated beverages are called both "soda" and "pop." Throughout the translation process, you'll likely make many decisions about which words to use. To save time and to ensure consistency, create an in-house glossary of these words so that next time your translation job will be easier when searching for the "just right" words.

Other communication tools. Along with translated documents, have additional ways of communicating with non-English speaking patients. This can be especially useful when communicating with patients who can't read in their native language or when translated materials or interpreters are not available. Communication tools include step-by-step illustrated instructions and books or cards with common medical phrases translated into other languages.

Translations help bridge communication between people who do not share a common language.

Sources to Learn More

Dollinger RK, 1992. *Pocket Medical Spanish*. Van Nuys, CA: Booksmythe. Available at http://www.booksmythe.com. Accessed January 18, 2004.

Hunt S, Bhopal R, 2003. "Self-reports in research with non-English speakers," *BMJ*, 237:352–3

McGee J, 1999. *Writing and Designing Print Materials for Beneficiaries: A Guide for State Medicaid Agencies.* HCFA Publication Number 10145. Baltimore, MD: Centers for Medicare & Medicaid Services, U.S. Department of Health and Human Services. (A second edition is forthcoming in 2004. For ordering information, contact Jeanne McGee, McGee & Evers Consulting, Inc., Vancouver, Washington, 360-574-4744, jmcgee@pacifier.com).

Multilingual glossary of technical and popular medical terms in nine European Languages. Available at http://allserv.rug.ac.be/~rvdstich/eugloss/welcome.html. Accessed January 28, 2004.

Neergaard L, 2003."Hospital struggle with growing language barrier: Inaccurate translation leads to medical errors," *Charlotte Observer*, Sept. 2.

Osborne H, 2000a. "In other words…when you truly need to find other words …working with medical interpreters," *On Call* magazine, 3(7):38–39. Available at http://www.healthliteracy.com. Accessed January 23, 2004. Information is adapted and reprinted with permission of *On Call* magazine. *On Call* is published by Boston Works, a division of the *Boston Globe*.

_____, 2000b. "In other words…pathways to understanding: Working with employees who speak English as a second language," *On Call* magazine, 3(1):38–39. Available at http://www.healthliteracy.com. Accessed January 23, 2004. Information is adapted and reprinted with permission of *On Call* magazine. *On Call* is published by Boston Works, a division of the *Boston Globe*.

United States Census 2000, "Language use and English-speaking ability: 2000," U.S. Department of Commerce, Economics and Statistics Administration. Available at http://factfinder.census.gov. Accessed January 24, 2004.

Universal Design in Print and on the Web

Starting Points

Universal design describes a concept of designing products, environments, and communications that not only considers the specific needs of people with physical disabilities, but also takes into account the more universal changes that everyone faces as they age. Curb cuts on sidewalks are an example of universal design. They not only help people in wheelchairs but also are valued by parents with baby strollers and travelers with wheeled suitcases.

In health communications, universal design is equally beneficial. For example, easy-to-see signs, easy-to-read brochures, and easy-to-use web sites are helpful to and appreciated by most everyone. "If a design works well for a person with a disability, it probably works better for everybody," says Valerie Fletcher, executive director of Adaptive Environments in Boston, MA.

Strategies, Ideas, and Suggestions

Assemble a team. It takes a team to design print and web-based materials that work for everyone. From the first idea to testing and production, work with a team that is committed to universal design. When writing patient education materials, for example, your team might include clinical and administrative staff, graphic designers, and "user/experts" who are patients or family members.

Include user/experts. User/experts represent the consumers you are designing for. Solicit their opinion as you design materials, and ask them about both usability and appeal. Almost always, user/experts are pleased to help as they know their opinions will make a difference.

Start by asking just one or two user/experts for their opinion. Continue this questioning until you have the information necessary to design for a larger population. Elicit feedback with open-ended questions such as, "How would this work best for you?" Also, explore effectiveness by asking about specific elements such as color combinations.

Balance opposing needs. Sometimes one person's needs and preferences are directly the opposite of someone else's. For example, a person with low vision may prefer reverse lettering—light print on a dark background—while a person with normal vision may prefer dark lettering on a light background. Find ways to accommodate both preferences in the critical elements of your design. For example, you might use reverse lettering in key parts of a brochure (such as the title and headings) while using standard lettering in the body of the text.

Font. Choose a font that is not overly stylized and does not vary too much from what people are used to seeing. People often have strong opinions about font. Some prefer serif fonts in which the letters have little "feet" or "wings." An example is Times New Roman, which is found in most word processing programs. Others favor sans serif fonts like Arial, which is a type of block lettering. While there is no clear-cut answer for which is best to use in print, many graphic designers recommend sans serif or a font called Verdana for websites and illuminated (Microsoft™ Power Point©) presentations.

Type size. For regular text, use a type size between 12 and 16 points. Type that is smaller than 12-point is hard for most people to see. Type that is larger than 16-point can result in more pages than most people want to read.

Line length. People with low vision may have difficulty when there are too many words on a line; people with cognitive impairments may have difficulty when there are too few. In general, most people prefer seven to twelve words in a line of continuous text. This relatively short line length can often be accomplished with columns (like in a newspaper), with two columns per page. Justify (line up evenly) the text on the left margin and keep the right margin ragged (uneven).

Pictures. Choose pictures that have sufficient contrast between foreground and background. Crop the pictures so that they have a clear border around a central image. When you include pictures on your website, provide descriptive text alongside graphic images as well as alternate text for those who cannot make use of the graphics at all. (To learn more about website design, go to Website Design on page 251.)

Paper finish. Glossy paper has a glare that can be difficult for people with impaired vision to see. To increase legibility, use matte paper for all your printed materials.

Illuminated presentations. To ensure that illuminated presentations (like slides and Microsoft™ Power Point©) are easy-to-see and easy-to-understand, use Verdana or a sans serif font like you would for website text. And have no more than five lines of text on each slide; each line should have no more than five words. This way, your audience will find it easier to read and better understand the information you are presenting.

Universal design describes a concept of designing products, environments, and communications that not only considers the specific needs of people with physical disabilities but also takes into account the more universal changes that everyone faces as they age.

Sources to Learn More

Adaptive Environments. Available at http://www.adaptenv.org. Accessed January 28, 2004.

Center for Universal Design, North Carolina State University. Available at http://www.design.ncsu.edu/cud/univ_design/ud.htm. Accessed January 28, 2004.

Osborne H, 2001. "In other words...communicating across a life span...universal design in print and web-based communication," *On Call* magazine, 4(1):34–35. Available at http://www.healthliteracy.com. Accessed January 22, 2004. Information is adapted and reprinted with permission of *On Call* magazine. *On Call* is published by Boston Works, a division of the *Boston Globe*.

Trace Center, College of Engineering, University of Wisconsin-Madison. Available at http://www.tracecenter.org. Accessed January 28, 2004.

Vision: Communicating with People who are Blind or have Limited Vision

Starting Points

People with visual problems may either be blind and totally without sight or legally blind and, even with corrective lenses, have restricted or limited vision. According to the American Foundation for the Blind, there are approximately 10 million blind and visually impaired people in the United States, with more than half aged 65 and older. Age-related macular degeneration accounts for almost 45% of all cases of low vision, according to the National Eye Institute.

Health facilities are required to accommodate the needs of people with vision problems. The 1990 Americans with Disabilities Act mandates that public facilities (like hospitals and health centers) provide reasonable accommodations for people who are blind. These facilities must provide information in large print, audiotape, Braille formats, or have someone available to read information aloud.

A person with vision problems may use hearing, touch, smell, and remaining vision to learn about the environment. For example, when a legally blind person goes into an unfamiliar building for a medical appointment, he or she may ask for specific directions to the office, locate stairways and offices by using a white cane or guide dog, and use any remaining vision to read room numbers and exit signs. Some people may also use Braille, which is a system of writing using six raised dots in various combinations to connote letters and numbers.

People who are blind may have trouble distinguishing one medication from another because pill bottles are often identical in shape and size. One way people with vision problems can tell the two medications apart is by putting one rubber band (or piece of tape) on the first bottle and two rubber bands (or pieces of tape) on the second. Another way is by asking pharmacists to put the different medications in two differently shaped containers. In addition, people with vision problems might keep one medication in the bedroom and another in the kitchen to keep track of which is which.

Strategies, Ideas, and Suggestions

Ask if the person wants assistance. The amount of assistance a person desires depends on the situation and his or her comfort in asking. Ask if a person wants help and, if so, find out how you can best be of assistance. The person may want descriptive or directional information such as identifying where objects are located within a room, or explaining any unusual sounds or noises. The person may also ask to walk with you, putting his or her hand through the crook of your elbow.

Some people, however, may choose not to reveal their blindness, especially at initial meetings. As a matter of practice you should ask all patients, "Would you like that information in any other format?" Talk with patients about function, rather than vision. Ask, for example, "How can I help you?" rather than "How much can you see?"

Introduce yourself and others. Identify yourself by name when you enter the room where there is a blind person. When a person with low vision comes in, introduce yourself and everyone else who is present. When someone leaves the room, communicate this information as well.

Use everyday words. Give clear, specific information and use common words, not medical jargon. Don't be afraid to use verbs such as "see" and "look;" they are a part of everyday speech.

Provide clear directions. Be specific and descriptive. When you refer a patient to a new facility, make sure that person is comfortable going to an unfamiliar location. One way you can help is by giving detailed directions that make use of landmarks. Be sure, however, you talk about "left" and "right" from the other person's perspective, not your own.

Written materials. By making a few accommodations and adjustments, written information can be helpful—even to people who have limited vision. Here's how:

- When using a computer, use a simple font and avoid italics or other stylized lettering. Increase the print size to at least 14-point; 16–18-point is preferable.

- Have a high contrast between the color of the foreground and background. Generally, this is black lettering on white or light paper.

- Use matte rather than glossy paper to reduce glare.

- Have margins that are at least an inch wide and increase line spacing from single space to at least one and a half spaces.

- As needed, enlarge materials when you reproduce them on a copier machine.

- When writing by hand, write in large-sized letters using thick felt tip markers. Use print or block lettering rather than script and avoid writing in all capital letters because this format is difficult to read.

Color. People with partial sight or color deficiencies may have trouble distinguishing between certain color combinations. Compensate for these difficulties by choosing colors that are drastically different in terms of their tone (basic color), lightness (how much light is reflected) and saturation (the intensity of color).

Non-visual cues. Talk with patients about non-visual sensory cues. For example, when teaching a person how to recognize signs of a wound infection, include the warning symptoms of oozing, swelling, tenderness, and sensation of heat in addition to redness. As well, help patients learn non-visual ways to accomplish tasks. For example, if a person is having difficulty seeing the numbers on a thermometer—even with a magnifier—let him or her know that a talking thermometer is available.

Media. Maintain a library of high-quality patient education audiotapes or CDs. Consider using videotapes or DVDs, but make sure that the narration adequately describes the visuals. For all media, have supplemental information available in a written format.

Signage. Use both Braille and large print (at least 16-point type) to identify offices, room numbers, departments, building directories, elevator call buttons, and elevator door jams (those panels by the door that indicate the floor number). Make sure printed signs have sufficient contrast between foreground and background and that the background of the sign contrasts with the wall color.

The amount of assistance a person desires depends on the situation and his or her comfort in asking. Ask if a person wants help and, if so, find out how you can best be of assistance.

Sources to Learn More

American Foundation for the Blind. Available at http://www.afb.org/default.asp. Accessed January 28, 2004.

Americans with Disabilities Act. Available at www.usdoj.gov/crt/ada/ada-hom1.htm. Accessed January 28, 2004.

Arditi A, 1999. *Making Text Legible: Designing for People with Partial Sight*, New York, NY: Lighthouse International.

_____, 1999. *Effective Color Contrast: Designing for People with Partial Sight and Color Deficiencies.* New York, NY: Lighthouse International.

National Eye Institute. Frequently asked questions about low vision. Available at http://www.nei.nih.gov/nehep/faqs.htm. Accessed February 22, 2004.

National Federation of the Blind. Available at http://www.nfb.org. Accessed January 28, 2004.

Osborne H, 2002. *Partnering with Patients To Improve Health Outcomes.* Gaithersburg, MD: Aspen Publishers, Inc. Information is adapted and reprinted with the author's permission.

_____, 2000a. "In other words...when vision is an issue...communicating with patients who are visually impaired," *On Call* magazine, 3(10):38–39. Available at http://www.healthliteracy.com. Accessed January 28, 2004. Information is adapted and reprinted with permission of *On Call* magazine. *On Call* is published by Boston Works, a division of the *Boston Globe.*

_____, 2000b. *Overcoming Communication Barriers in Patient Education.* Gaithersburg, MD: Aspen Publishers, Inc. Information is adapted and reprinted with the author's permission.

Visuals

Starting Points

Visuals include artwork like photographs, anatomic diagrams, simple line drawings, cartoons, and decorative illustrations. You may commission a graphic artist to draw something for you or, instead, find what you need in a clip art collection. Regardless of which visuals you use and how you acquire them, when used well visuals enhance written health materials by illustrating key points and making documents more attractive and appealing.

Visuals can also aid comprehension. For example, one study looked at the effect of cartoon illustrations on compliance and comprehension of the wound care instructions that patients are given at discharge from an Emergency Department (ED). The conclusion of this randomized, controlled study suggests "that cartoon illustrations are an effective strategy for conveying information and may improve compliance with ED release instructions" (Delp and Jones, 1996).

Learners of all abilities appreciate visuals. Those who are visual learners, for example, learn best when seeing pictures of what they need to do. Others, including people with limited literacy or language skills, can understand new concepts more easily when information is in pictures and not just words. And visuals are appealing, memorable, and of interest to most everyone.

Herb, a 66-year-old general contractor, had a major heart attack five years ago. His doctor performed an emergency coronary angiography to examine the blood vessels and chambers of his heart. After the procedure, Herb's doctor gave him a simple line drawing of the heart and arteries. She then colored in where each artery was blocked and wrote alongside how much each was occluded.

Seeing so clearly what was wrong, Herb readily agreed to participate in a cardiac rehabilitation program and change his diet and exercise habits. He did so well that he was asked to speak with other patients who had just been diagnosed with cardiovascular disease. To Herb's surprise and disappointment, not one of the more than 100 people he spoke with had ever been given a "heart picture" like his. Herb often hears people say how these types of drawings could have helped them better understand their diagnosis and treatment recommendations.

Strategies, Ideas, and Suggestions

Visual appeal and tone. Choose good quality visuals that not only are appealing but also illustrate key points. Pictures of familiar and interesting people, objects, or places generally work well. Purely decorative designs, however, are sometimes confusing and distracting. Make sure to maintain the quality of your visuals by not reproducing copies of copies (of copies of copies).

Visuals, even more than words, can express emotion. Make sure to select ones that are appropriate to your subject matter. For example, you might use humorous, cartoon-like characters when writing about well-baby care, but chose more subdued illustrations when writing about a serious diagnosis.

Mixing and matching formats. Although it's tempting to include many different types of visuals (like photographs, anatomical illustrations, and simple line drawings), aim for a more unified and consistent look by using just one or two. For example, if you are creating a one-page handout about neck and back exercises, you might want to have just simple line drawings (all by the same artist) of each exercise rather than add anatomic diagrams and photographs of proper posture.

Include pictures your readers can relate to. Select visuals of people, places, and objects that are consistent with your readers' culture, age, and gender. You can demonstrate sensitivity and respect by choosing visuals that not only are realistic but also show people at their best. Make sure, as well, that your artwork is as current as your text. Pictures of telephones with curlicue phone cords may be more relevant to someone of my generation than they are to teenagers accustomed to cordless technology.

Keep in mind that colors and symbols are sometimes "culturally-bound" and may have different meaning to readers from other parts of the world. For example, a picture of a pill bottle alongside a knife and fork may be intended to show that medication should be taken with meals. But for those from countries where food is taken by hand from a common serving bowl, this symbol may have no meaning or relevance.

Parts of the body. When writing about just one part of the body, such as the spleen, it's tempting to show only this aspect of the anatomy. Try, instead, to include at least one picture of the whole human body with the spleen clearly identified. This way, readers can see how large the spleen is and where it is located. Also, you avoid "disembodied body parts" which may be upsetting, especially to people traumatized by violence or war.

Combine pictures and text. Pictures alone are seldom sufficient. To ensure that everyone who sees your written material understands its visuals, include simply worded captions beneath each one. These captions not only help readers know what they're looking at but also reinforce key messages and actions.

Show restraint. Readers may get distracted or confused by abundant and ornate visuals. Keep your visual information as clutter-free as possible, showing only the level of detail you truly need. While in Herb's case (see above), it is important to include all the major arteries, a more general material about the benefits of exercise may not need that level of cardiac detail.

With the Internet, people have easy access to clip art libraries of photographs, drawings, anatomical drawings, and cartoon-like figures. Some clip art is free; others require that you pay a user or license fee. My bias is to show restraint when choosing clip art. Just because you can find a lot of pictures doesn't mean you need to use them all.

Step-by-step instructions. When you write step-by-step instructions, number the steps and add pictures of the correct way to perform each action. This way, readers have words, pictures, and numbers to help them learn exactly what to do. (To see an example, go to Pictographs on page 175.)

Visuals as interactive teaching tools. Just like Herb's physician did with his heart picture, you can personalize visuals by circling, highlighting, writing on, or otherwise marking what patients need to know. You can also encourage patients to interact with visuals by placing check-off boxes or fill-in-the-blanks next to illustrated instructions.

Pain scales. These are tools that patients can use to express the intensity of their pain. While sometimes pain scales are just words ("rate your pain on a scale from 1 to 10"), other times pain is also shown in pictures. (To learn more, go to http://www3.us.elsevierhealth.com/WOW/faces.html.)

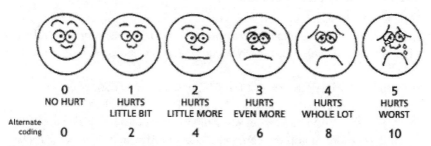

Figure 1.1. FACES Pain Rating Scale. Source: From Wong D. L., Hochenberry-Eaton M., Wilson D., Winkelstein M. L., Schwartz P. Wongs Essentials of Pediatric Nursing, ed. 6, St. Louis, 2001, p. 1301. Copyrighted by Mosby, Inc. Reprinted by permission.

For people with disabilities. Consider the needs of all your readers, including those with visual or cognitive disabilities. Make your visuals easy to see by having a lot of contrast. Generally, this means black ink on white or very light-colored paper. Don't rely solely on color to convey your message, however. Some people cannot differentiate between two shades of the same color or may not be able to see colors at all. As well, avoid decorative backgrounds like watermarks or washes, which make it hard for people to know where to focus their attention.

Field test. Just as with all other forms of communication, make sure your readers understand, accept, and can use your visual information. Ask your intended audience for their feedback and confirm that your illustrations, colors, and symbols are appealing and informative. (To learn more about feedback, go to Feedback: Interviews and Focus Groups on page 57.)

Regardless of what visuals you use and how you acquire them, when used well visuals can enhance your written health materials by illustrating key points and making documents more attractive and appealing to read.

Sources to Learn More

AMC Cancer Research Center, 1994. *Beyond the Brochure: Alternative Approaches to Effective Health Communication.* Center for Disease Control and Prevention. Available at http://www.cdc.gov/cancer/nbccedp. Accessed January 24, 2004.

National Cancer Institute, 1994. *Clear & Simple: Developing Effective Print Materials for Low-Literate Readers.* National Institutes of Health.

Delp C, Jones J, 1996. "Communicating information to patients: The use of cartoon illustrations to improve comprehension of instructions," *Academic Emergency Medicine,* 3(3):264–270.

Doak CC, Doak LG, Root JH, 1996. *Teaching Patients with Low Literacy Skills,* 2nd ed. Philadelphia, PA: J.B. Lippincott Company.

FACES Pain Rating Scale, Wong on the Web. Available at http://www3.us. elsevierhealth.com/WOW/faces.html. Accessed January 28, 2004.

Farwell T, (date unavailable). "Visual, auditory, kinesthetic: Which is your child?," *Family Education Network.* Available at http://familyeducation.com/ article/0,1120,3-605,00.html. Accessed January 28, 2004.

Graham RB, 2002. "The purpose of pain scales," *InteliHealth.* Available at www.intelihealth.com/IH/ihtPrint/WSIHW000/29721/32087.html?hide=t& k=basePri. Accessed January 28, 2004.

Health Communication Materials Network. Available at http://www.hcmn.org/index.htm. Accessed January 28, 2004.

McGee J, 1999. *Writing and Designing Print Materials for Beneficiaries: A Guide for State Medicaid Agencies.* HCFA Publication Number 10145. Baltimore, MD: Centers for Medicare & Medicaid Services, U.S. Department of Health and Human Services. (A second edition is forthcoming in 2004. For ordering information, contact Jeanne McGee, McGee & Evers Consulting, Inc., Vancouver, Washington, 360-574-4744, jmcgee@pacifier.com).

Osborne H, 2003. "In other words…communicating about health with new immigrants," *On Call* magazine, 6(10):16–17. Available at http://www. healthliteracy.com. Accessed January 23, 2004. Information is adapted and reprinted with permission of *On Call* magazine. *On Call* is published by Boston Works, a division of the *Boston Globe.*

Scientific and Technical Information Simply Put, 1999. Atlanta, GA: Centers for Disease Control and Prevention.

Website Design

Starting Points

Many people today go to websites when they want to learn about health topics. A recent study found that searching for medical information is one of the top ten most popular Internet activities (UCLA, 2003). In fact, health websites have become so popular that many people go online even before consulting with their medical providers.

To meet the needs of people of all ages, abilities, disabilities, and levels of technical savvy, websites must be designed in user-friendly ways. This means that people with limited literacy or language skills can read the text; those with physical or cognitive disabilities can use the site with adaptive equipment like screen readers, special keyboards, and voice input devices; and people with limited technical skills, older computers, and slow Internet connections can access and navigate the website. The best way to know if your site achieves these goals is through usability testing.

> Usability testing is a must. What's intuitive to a web developer may not be for the end user who has never seen the site before. You can never be sure that people get to where they want to be unless you test the site with the folks who will be using it.
>
> —Lorna Patrick, patient information specialist at the National Cancer Institute's Office of Education and Special Initiatives

Strategies, Ideas, and Suggestions

Usability. Usability is "the measure of the quality of a user's experience when interacting with a product or system—whether a website, a software application, mobile technology, or any user-operated device." Usability looks at a combination of factors that affect the user's experience, including ease of learning, efficiency of use, memorability, error frequency and severity, and subjective satisfaction (Usability.gov).

Test for usability throughout the web development process. Ask intended users (people likely to use your website) to try your site and watch as they figure out what to click and where to go. Pay attention, as well, to what users have difficulty with.

Web development takes a team. It takes a team of people and perspectives to develop usable and useful websites. While one person may assume more than one role, web development teams should at least include:

- a site owner who commissions the site, authorizes budget, and has ultimate veto-power
- content expert(s) who determine the information to include
- web developer(s) who are technical experts

- a site-manger who coordinates all aspects of web development including fixing problems, reviewing materials, and otherwise making sure the site remains "ship-shape."

Navigation pages. These are the basic feature pages that users expect, including:

- Home—an opening page that welcomes and orients users to the site
- About us—has information about the sponsoring organization
- Links—contains print and online resources to learn more
- Contact us—provides an email link, phone number, and street address. On my websites, I encourage users to contact me with their comments and feedback. Not only is it nice to get their positive comments but user feedback also informs me about problems to fix, like broken links or pages that don't open.

Content pages. These pages go beyond the basics of navigation pages. Content pages generally have more detailed and lengthy information (like articles and reports) that users may print out rather than just read from the screen. Given that users may print just some, not all, of the original document, you may want to add identifying headers on each page rather than just posting material "as is."

Readability, layout, and design. Web pages, especially navigation pages, should be easy to read and use. Use plain language with common words, short phrases or simple sentences, and paragraphs that are just two to three sentences long. Also, make sure to place the most important who, what, why, when, and how information at the top of each page as users do not always scroll down.

As well, web pages should look appealing and have plenty of white space (blank areas), headers, and bullet points. They also should be simply designed. A too busy web page not only is distracting but also can confuse users as to where to go and what to do.

Keep information up-to-date. Review your web content on a regular basis. At a minimum, you should do this once a year, but much more often when there is new information, research, or changes in practice. Let users know how current your site is by including the date it was last reviewed or updated.

Visuals and colors. While graphics, photos, logos, and other designs add visual appeal, users might turn off the visuals because they can't see them or because the visuals take too long to download. Design your site to work equally well with and without visuals. You can do this by having alternative text (alt text) that describes in words what the visuals show. For example, a map of the world would have the accompanying alt text, "map of the world." Don't rely just on color to communicate a message. Instead, include text like saying "click here to enter" rather than just having a green button.

Test your technology. Even though you may have the latest technology, design your site to work equally as well for those with dial-up connections, low-resolution monitors, and older browsers. You might test how well your site works by looking at it on an older computer that does not have all the latest "bells and whistles."

Accessible to people with disabilities. Accessible websites are not just the right thing to do, they are also often mandated by law. The U.S. Federal Rehabilitation Act, Section 508, requires that all federal departments and agencies have sites that are accessible by people with disabilities. Though not mandated, the World Wide Web Consortium Web Accessibility Initiative also sets international guidelines and standards for accessibility. Here are some ways to design accessible websites:

- Use sufficiently large type that people can see. Also, avoid busy backgrounds that may distract or confuse people. As a general rule, follow the same design principles for your website as you do for printed information.

- Make sure that people can navigate without a mouse by using only keyboard controls like "page up" and "page down." This is needed not only for people who use mouth sticks or head sticks, but also for those with hand tremors or other fine-motor difficulties.

- Provide alternative text (written description) for all images on your web page. This helps people with visual impairments or those with slow Internet connections who might turn off the graphic feature from their web browsers. An example is "picture of a pill bottle" as a text alternative to a picture of a pill bottle.

- Make sure that your site is compatible with adaptive technology such as screen readers and voice browsers that read aloud information displayed on the monitor.

- Avoid using columns and tables and instead write materials in a text format. This is because some adaptive technology reads across entire lines rather than going column-by-column.

- Provide alternatives to online forms. When you require formatted information, such as a registration form, have other ways that people can complete this task. For example, include a phone number for people to call instead of filling out the online form.

- Assess the accessibility of your website. One way to do this is with automated evaluation tools like the "Bobby" from WatchFire™. Tools like these can help determine if your site does *not* meet accessibility guidelines but sometimes are overwhelming when pinpointing specific problems. From experience, I've learned to add a dose of common sense when interpreting automated evaluation tools. Another way to assess accessibility is to test your website with actual users. They truly are the best ones to judge whether your site is useful, informative, and accessible.

It is important that websites be "user-friendly," meaning that people of all ages, abilities, disabilities, and levels of technical savvy can access and use them.

Sources to Learn More

Bobby. Available at http://bobby.watchfire.com/bobby/html/en/index.jsp. Accessed January 28, 2004.

Fox S, Fallows D, 2003. *Internet Health Resources,* Pew Internet & American Life Project. Available at http://www.pewinternet.org. Accessed January 28, 2004.

Nielsen J, 2000. *Designing Web Usability.* Indianapolis, IN: New Riders Publishing.

Osborne H, 2003. "In other words... making sure your web site is accessible," *On Call* magazine, 6(4):16–17. Available at http://www.healthliteracy.com. Accessed January 22, 2004. Information is adapted and reprinted with permission of *On Call* magazine. *On Call* is published by Boston Works, a division of the *Boston Globe.*

UIAccess, Web accessibility evaluation tools need people. Available at http://www.uiaccess.com/evaltools.html. Accessed January 28, 2004.

Use.it.com. Available at http://www.useit.com. Accessed January 28, 2004.

Section 508: The Road to Accessibility. Available at www.section508.gov. Accessed January 28, 2004.

Setting Priorities for Retirement Years (SPRY) Foundation. Available at http://www.spry.org/index.html. Accessed January 28, 2004.

University of California, Los Angeles, 2003. Internet report: Surveying the digital future year three. Available at http://ccp.ucla.edu/pdf/UCLA-Internet-Report-Year-Three.pdf. Accessed January 28, 2004.

Usability.gov, National Cancer Institute. Available at http://usability.gov/index.html. Accessed January 28, 2004.

Web Accessibility Initiative (WAI). Available at www.w3.org/WAI/Resources. Accessed January 28, 2004.

Word Choice

Starting Points

Health professionals invest many years learning a new language of specialized medical words and terms that are considered by many to be jargon. Patients, however, are likely not as familiar with these words. Perhaps they have limited literacy or language skills and find these new words hard to read or to understand. Or maybe patients simply have never before had reason to learn these words. Instead, patients may prefer and better understand more common "everyday," "lay language," "plain language," or "living room" words.

Health professionals do not need to avoid all medical words just because patients are unfamiliar with them. A recent study found that patients sometimes prefer medical words, feeling these words legitimize their illnesses or conditions (Ogden, et al., 2003). Lay language, however, can help patients more easily learn about the tasks and behaviors they need to do. Often, a good compromise is for health professionals to give patients the correct medical terminology along with a simply worded explanation.

Sometimes relying solely on lowering the reading level of materials can lead to many other problems. When attempting to improve communication, I notice in our literacy programs that it is almost a point of pride for students to say 'I have diabetes' as opposed to 'I got sugar.' This just goes to show the complexity of health communications.

—From Debbie Yoho, Executive Director of the Greater
Columbia Literacy Council in South Carolina

Strategies, Ideas, and Suggestions

Readability assessments. The Fry, SMOG, and many other reading grade-level formulas assess reading difficulty by counting the number of syllables in words and the number of words in sentences. This means that documents with mostly one- and two-syllable words score at lower grade levels than those with a lot of three or more syllables words. These formulas, however, do not take into account other readability factors such as personal relevance. Indeed, a person with cancer is likely to know the word "chemotherapy" despite its many syllables. (To learn more about assessing readability, go to Assessing Readability on page 13.)

State your message simply. Unless you need a specific medical word (like "chemotherapy" in the example above), use mostly one- and two-syllable words that people already know. For example, use "choice" instead of "decision," "often" instead of "commonly," and "rules" instead of "regulations."

When "simple" words aren't simple. Sometimes even commonly used words like "may," "might," and "suggest" are difficult to understand. This often happens when describing risk. While the phrase "this treatment might help" can mean to a scientist that there is no conclusive evidence, it can be interpreted as "this treatment will help" to a patient desperate for hope. (To learn more about risk communication, go to Risk Communication on page 191.)

Teach necessary new words and terms. Don't avoid words just because they are unfamiliar or difficult; sometimes they are the best ones to use. When you introduce a new word like "childproofing," define it simply perhaps by saying "making sure your home is safe for small children." Then add an example and maybe also a picture, such as of a baby gate or electrical outlet cover. You might also want to add a phonetic (fo-NE-tik) spelling to help readers pronounce difficult new words.

Sometimes people know the individual words you are using but do not understand their meaning in a health context. For example, the phrase "drawing blood" has nothing to do with crayons. As well, people may think they know what your words mean but are incorrect, such as assuming that decongestants are for digestion. As with all forms of health communication, make sure that you and patients correctly understand one another.

Consistency. Use the same words throughout your document, practice, and continuum of care. This means always saying and writing "bandage" and not also using "dressing" or "gauze." It also means using the same form of a word like "surgery" and not "surgeries" and "surgical procedures."

Acronyms and other new "words." Acronyms are made-up words using the first letters from each word in a phrase. Sometimes they sound familiar like "CAT" for "Computed/Computerized Axial Tomography." Other times, they create a new "word" (which really isn't a word) like "ADL" which stands for "activities of daily living." Whether or not they sound familiar, acronyms can be hard to understand. To help, write out the entire term the first time you use it and put the acronym in parentheses alongside it. For example, "Blood pressure (BP)."

Jargon. Medical jargon refers to technical terms and phrases used to communicate complex information. While jargon may be familiar and useful to health professionals, patients and families often do not understand these words and phrases. For example, in healthcare the term "unremarkable" generally means "you're fine" while the term "positive" may mean you're not. Jargon like this means quite the opposite of what most people expect.

Concepts, categories, and value judgments. These types of words, though familiar, can be difficult to understand because patients may not have the knowledge or experience to know what they mean.

- Concept words describe general ideas or abstract concepts that readers cannot see or touch and include terms like "wellness" and "health status."
- Categories are groups of things which, like concepts, are intangible such as "benefits" and "risks."
- Value judgment words describe amounts or thresholds that readers must determine for themselves and include words like "rarely" and "often."

Contractions. Be cautious when using contractions like "don't" and "you'll." Though they sound friendly and conversational, people with limited reading skills or those just learning English may not understand them. Instead of contractions, write out the full words as in "do not" and "you will."

Homonyms. These are words that sound alike, may or may not be spelled the same way, but have very different meanings. Healthcare uses a lot of homonyms like "stool," "gait," and "plant." Be aware that patients can easily misinterpret homonyms. As with all new words, make sure to clarify exactly what they mean.

Idioms. These are phrases that mean something quite different from their actual words. Generally, idioms have special meaning to people from a certain country or culture. This meaning, however, may be unfamiliar to outsiders. Because most health materials are written for a general (not local) reading audience, try and avoid using idioms like "feeling blue" and "heads up."

Words change over time. For example, what was once called "senility" is now referred to as "dementia" or "Alzheimer's Disease." Older adults, for example, may be more comfortable with words they've always heard rather than new terms they are expected to learn.

Substitute word lists. Rather than struggle each time you want to find a "just right" word, create a substitute word list of terms you find acceptable. Ask your colleagues to help and together build a department-wide (or facility-wide) list of words to use. To speed up this process, you might build on already existing substitute word lists (some of these are starred in the "Sources to Learn More" section below).

Clarify understanding. Sometimes people think they know what words mean, but they really don't. Other times, people are not comfortable saying they don't understand. Make sure that patients truly understand the words and terms you are using. For example, when you say "take orally," let patients know that this means taking the medicine by mouth. As with all forms of health communication, ask patients to tell you in their own words what they understand. You might begin by saying, "Some people have trouble understanding the word. ... What does this word mean to you?"

Health professionals do not need to avoid all medical words just because patients are unfamiliar with them.

Sources to Learn More

*Deciphering medspeak, Medical Library Association. Available at http://www.mlanet.org/resources/medspeak/medspeaka d.html. Accessed January 29, 2004.

Doak CC, Doak LG, Root JH, 1996. *Teaching Patients with Low Literacy Skills*, 2nd ed. Philadelphia, PA: J.B. Lippincott Company.

Ellner A, Hoey A, Frisch L, 2003. "Speak up! Can patients get better at working with their doctors?," *BMJ*, 327:303–304.

Hochhauser M, 2003. "Concepts, categories, and value judgments in informed consent forms," *IRB: Ethics & Human Research*, 25(5):7–10.

Hunt S, Bhopal R, 2003. "Self-reports in research with non-English speakers," *BMJ*, 237:352–353.

Lukoschek P, Fazzari M, Marantz P, 2003. "Patient and physician factors predict patients' comprehension of health information," *Patient Education and Counseling*, 50:201–210.

Norris P, Bird K, Kirifi J et al, 2002. "Talking the talk," *Prescriber Update*, 23(1):10–11.

Ogden J et al, 2003. "What's in a name? An experimental study of patients' views of the impact and function of a diagnosis," *Family Practice*, 20(3):248–253.

Osborne H, 2004. "In other words...the ethics of simplicity," *On Call* magazine, 7(2):16–17. Available at http://www.healthliteracy.com. Accessed March 12, 2004. Information is adapted and reprinted with permission of *On Call* magazine. *On Call* is published by Boston Works, a division of the *Boston Globe*.

_____, 2000. "In other words...when it's time to choose...thinking about the right words," *On Call* magazine, 3(11):34–35. Available at http://www.health-literacy.com. Accessed January 22, 2004. Information is adapted and reprinted with permission of *On Call* magazine. *On Call* is published by Boston Works, a division of the *Boston Globe*.

PlainLanguage.gov. Available at http://www.plainlanguage.gov. Accessed January 26, 2004.

*Plain Language Principles and Thesaurus for Making HIPAA Privacy Notices More Readable, HRSA of the U.S. Department of Health and Human Services, Washington, D.C. Available at http://www.hrsa.gov/language.htm. Accessed January 22, 2004. (Includes "Thesaurus of Plain Language Words and Phrases for HIPAA Notices of Privacy Practices.")

Scientific and Technical Information Simply Put, 1999. Atlanta, GA: Centers for Disease Control and Prevention.

*University of Utah, Health Science Center's "Substitute word list." Available at www.med.utah.edu/pated/authors/substitute2.html. Accessed January 29, 2004.

*Includes a substitute word list or glossary

X-tras

Starting Points

X-tras (or "extras" for spelling enthusiasts) make programs unique and yours. Always creative and usually fun, extras include "far-out" ideas, "out-of the-box" thinking, and "off-the-wall" communication strategies that can help people better understand health information.

Extras aren't just entertainment. Indeed, they are rooted in the philosophy that people have more capacity to learn when they are relaxed and having fun. Additionally, most extras are multimodal and appeal to people's varied learning styles of seeing, doing, and interacting. Extras are effective with audiences of all ages and abilities including health professionals, patients, students, and the general public.

Creativity drives many of these extras. Whether inspired and developed by just one person, a whole department, or the entire organization, creative extras can provide services and tools to meet today's healthcare challenges.

The Southern Illinois Professional Development Center (a program that teaches teachers of adult education programs) held a "Trash Sculptures for Health Literacy" contest. Its purpose was "to celebrate imagination and creativity while increasing awareness of recycling and health literacy." Focusing on the theme of Family Health, groups of adult education students and their teachers created sculptures using only recyclables like aluminum cans, junk mail, and bubble wrap.

Contest entries were more diverse and creative than the organizers ever imagined. One group created a "Healthy City" landscape showing where health centers, grocery stores, pharmacies, and other health resources are located in their area. Another group built a "Healthy Home" including ways to keep toxic household materials out of the reach of small children. And a third group created their own version of a "Food Pyramid" complete with realistic-looking food and accompanying brochures about healthy nutrition. Indeed, everyone was a contest winner. In addition to prizes and bragging rights, all participants won by learning about ways to keep themselves and their families safe and healthy.

—From Colleen Potter and Sarah Goldammer, contest organizers
and educational training specialists at the Southern Illinois
Professional Development Center in Edwardsville, Illinois

Strategies, Ideas, and Suggestions

Getting creative. Admittedly, some people are naturally more creative than others. But even those who believe they are not creative can learn to think in more innovative ways. When I supervised occupational therapy students, for example, we often faced clinical situations in which traditional interventions didn't work or didn't work well. To help the students come up with alternative treatment solutions, I asked them to participate in two creativity exercises, "making the strange familiar" and "making the familiar strange."

Using just common household items, these exercises helped the students think of old problems in new ways. Together, we then applied this type of creative thinking to our very real clinical dilemmas.

Creativity starts with you. Even one person can make a creative difference. What's needed is passion for an idea, commitment to follow through, and willingness to take a risk. In fact, ideas like the Trash Sculpture contest, Colossal Colon (see page 164), and even Health Literacy Month were all started by just one or two people who had creative ideas and the determination to follow through. (To learn more about the colossal colon go to http://www.prevent-cancer.org/colossalcolon/Tour/Wat_colon.htm. To learn more about Health Literacy Month go to http://www.healthliteracy.com.)

Encouraging participation. Make it easy and comfortable for people to participate in innovative projects. Give them permission to be silly; supply needed materials, encouragement, and support; and offer your sincere appreciation and thanks. If and when you meet resistance from people who are skeptical or unwilling to participate, offer them assurance and encouragement. But also be willing to accept their refusal.

Personal relevance. Beyond being entertaining, extras should relate to people's concerns and interests. While you as the creator may be clear about the value of an innovative project, be prepared to talk about how participating can help others.

The Trash Sculpture contest, for example, was on the theme of family health because this issue is personally relevant to most adult education students. By making sculptures, the students learned important lessons such as where health facilities are in their neighborhood, how to keep their homes safe, and which foods are healthy to eat. At the same time, the students used reading, writing, and math skills to figure out how to construct their three-dimensional food pyramid.

Tie in with program goals. Extras shouldn't be superfluous but instead be designed to support and enhance program goals. Health Literacy Month, for example, was created to amplify the need to raise awareness about the importance of understandable health information. The Trash Sculpture contest was designed as a fun way for adult learners to learn health information they will use in their daily lives.

Expressive therapies. Some forms of multimodal communication are not "extra" at all. Indeed, expressive modalities like art therapy, music therapy, pet therapy, drama, gardening, and even puppetry are often essential treatment components. For example, Marge Schneider, an educator and expressive puppeteer at Hospice and Palliative Care of Connecticut, uses handheld puppets in her work with patients in hospice care. She finds that the puppets not only help break down communication barriers (often resulting from depression or dementia) but also stimulate conversations and promote laughter, creativity, and joy.

Know your audience. Whether your innovative idea is geared more for students, patients, health professionals, or the general public, learn about your intended audience. Know about their literacy, language, culture, and learning needs. Be sensitive, as well, to people's capacity for humor, tolerance for uncertainty, and willingness to try something innovative and new.

Time, money, and support. Extra ideas are seldom in the budget. Almost always, it takes a dose of creativity to get needed resources—especially of time and money. Let internal and external funders know how this project can help generate income (such as by enrolling new patients or students) or reduce expenses (like cutting the cost of recidivism). Consider partnering with like-minded groups or asking local foundations or corporations for grants to help sponsor your project.

ting the cost of recidivism). Consider partnering with like-minded groups or asking local foundations or corporations for grants to help sponsor your project.

Just like most initiatives, extras do best when they have the full support of influential leaders. Make it easy for others to support your innovative project by showing how it supports the organization's mission and strategic plan.

Build on small successes. Big projects don't necessarily start that way. Many times, a cautious approach works best—especially with untested methods or ideas. You might want to try your creative idea in just one department or setting, and then look critically at what works and what doesn't. Sometimes, an idea you think will be terrific falls flat while another that you think uninspired turns out to be a phenomenal success. Your job is to look for the extra special difference between the two.

Whether inspired and developed by just one person, a whole department, or the entire organization, creative extras can provide services and tools to meet today's healthcare challenges.

Sources to Learn More

Colossal Colon. Available at http://www.preventcancer.org/colossalcolon/Tour/what_colon.htm. Accessed January 29, 2004.

Expressive Puppetry. Available at www.expressivepuppetry.com. Accessed January 29, 2004.

Gilmartin MJ, 1999. "Creativity: The fuel of innovation," *Nursing Administration Quarterly*, 23(2):1–8.

Health Literacy Month. Available at http:www.healthliteracymonth.org. Accessed January 29, 2004.

Marks N, 2003. "Getting animated about medicine," *BMJ*, 327:1234.

You: Empathy and Humanity

Starting Points

In addition to knowledge, skills, and experiences, you bring "you" to each patient encounter. "You" includes empathy—a sensitivity to another person's feelings, thoughts, and experiences. "You" also includes humanity—responding to patients in a sensitive and caring manner, much as you would want to be cared for yourself.

Empathy and humanity go a long way to improve health communication. When patients feel valued and listened to, they likely will relax and be more receptive to learning new health information, even when that news is scary or sad. But when patients feel they are being treated in an impersonal or judgmental manner, they may well "tune out" and not fully process what their providers are saying or asking them to do.

Ken's son Chuck has many moles. When Chuck was 12 years old, his doctor biopsied two of his moles in a rather unpleasant procedure. A few days later, in a hurried phone call on a stormy New Year's Eve afternoon, the doctor called Ken with the test results. "I just received a report that your son has melanoma. We need to remove it right away." Not expecting the call that day and startled by the bad news, Ken's first thought was of the unpleasant biopsy. When Ken asked, "What happens if you don't remove it?" he expected to hear about treatment alternatives. Ken was dumbfounded when the doctor said, "Then your son only has eight months to live."

More than 20 years later, Ken vividly remembers this call. While thankful that Chuck's melanoma was successfully removed (by another doctor), Ken remains upset about what he feels was an insensitive, ill-timed, and thoughtless manner for this physician to have broken the bad news.

Thanks to Ken for sharing his story about Chuck.

Strategies, Ideas, Suggestions

Develop rapport. Set a tone for good communication by developing rapport with each patient. In office appointments, you can begin by briefly chatting about non-medical matters and then asking patients what they want to focus on today. When talking about diagnosis and treatment, find out how much information patients want to know and to what extent they are willing to participate in decision-making.

Actions and timing. Empathy is conveyed as much by actions as it is with words. Whether meeting in person or talking over the phone, use eye contact, body posture, and tone of voice to let patients know they have your full attention. As well, make sure patients are fully focused on what you are saying. In retrospect, the phone call between Ken and the doctor was ill-timed. The doctor was obviously rushed and even commented that he was calling from a pay phone in a rainy parking lot. Ken, in turn, was distracted by a houseful of New Year's Eve company.

Empathetic responses. Good health communication includes more than just clinical facts. It also includes empathic statements that acknowledge patient's feelings, concerns, and actions. The acronym NURS (Gordon, 2002) summarizes these responses:

- Name the feeling. For example, "You look (sad, frightened, …). Is that how you feel?"
- Understand and legitimize the feeling. For example, "It's understandable that you feel…."
- Respect coping efforts. For example, "You're doing the right thing by…."
- Support and partner with the patient. For example, "I look forward to helping you with…."

Pacing. Get your cues from patients about how quickly or slowly to present information. In Ken's case, the doctor rapidly jumped to the grimmest news possible. In replaying this conversation, Ken says he would have preferred it if the doctor had eased his concerns about the needed excision. Only if and when Ken raises the issue of long-term prognosis should the doctor address it.

Personal experiences. Some patients are comforted when their providers share a personal experience, such as a time when they were in a situation similar to the patient's. Before disclosing personal information, however, make sure the patient and family are receptive to you doing so. While some might find your openness helpful and supportive, others may feel that your experience is too much for them to deal with now. As well, consider your motives and make sure that you are revealing personal information solely for the patient's benefit.

Hope. Almost universally, patients want hope. Even when dealing with progressive illnesses, patients and families appreciate it when their providers offer encouragement and support their goals. Says Ken of a much more empathetic provider, "She didn't give up hope for us. We respond to hope."

> *When patients feel valued and listened to, they are apt to relax and therefore be more receptive to learning new health information, even when that news is scary or sad.*

Sources to Learn More

Gordon GH, 2002. "Care not cure: Dialogues at the transition," *Journal of Clinical Outcomes Management*, 9(12):677–681.

Osborne H, 2002. "In other words...communicating with families about end-of-life decisions," *On Call* magazine, 5(8):30–31. Available at http://www.healthliteracy.com. Accessed January 27, 2004. Information is adapted and reprinted with permission of *On Call* magazine. *On Call* is published by Boston Works, a division of the *Boston Globe*.

———, 2001. "In other words...know when to speak and when to listen...communicating with people who are anxious or angry." *On Call* magazine, 4(8):34–35. Available at http://www.healthliteracy.com. Accessed January 27, 2004. Information is adapted and reprinted with permission of *On Call* magazine. *On Call* is published by Boston Works, a division of the *Boston Globe*.

———, 1999. "In other words...finding out what you need to know...the importance of better interviewing skills," *On Call* magazine, 2(12):42–43. Available at http://www.healthliteracy.com. Accessed January 27, 2004. Information is adapted and reprinted with permission of *On Call* magazine. *On Call* is published by Boston Works, a division of the *Boston Globe*.

Zest and Pizzazz

Starting Points

Zest and pizzazz is about the commitment and passion you bring to health literacy. It is also about the energy that sustains and motivates you. Admittedly, it's fairly easy to remain enthusiastic about your work when there are obvious signs of success as when colleagues rave about a health literacy workshop you organized or patients beam with understanding when you drew pictures or used models to explain their disease process. But it can be much harder maintaining the momentum when you have to explain, yet again, what health literacy is and why it is important. Or when you have to deal with colleagues or supervisors who don't "get it" and continue to communicate with patients in ways that are not effective, empathetic, or understandable.

As a health literacy advocate, remember why you do this work. Whether your motivation is personal, professional, or both, appreciate that health literacy is everyone's responsibility. If you don't improve health communication, who will?

Strategies, Ideas, and Suggestions

Find your passion. Health literacy is seldom in anyone's job description. To have the energy to keep going, remember why health literacy matters. You may recall a personal experience as a patient or family member when health communication worked exceptionally well or particularly badly. Or you may remember a patient who stared blankly when you gave a brochure and another who grinned with understanding when you drew a picture. Zest and pizzazz start with knowing why you are passionate about health literacy.

Take risks. Health literacy is a fairly new concept. Figuring out how you can make a difference may, at times, feel like going on a trip without a roadmap. For some, it is exciting to lead the way so others can follow. For others, it is uncomfortable to venture into the unknown.

If, like me, you are willing to take risks, then health literacy means having the gusto and energy to try the untried. Sometimes what we try works. Sometimes it doesn't. Regardless of the outcome, we always learn something new.

Develop a support network. It's hard to remain enthusiastic when you feel as if you are the only health literacy advocate at your organization. To stay committed and enthusiastic, seek a network of others who share your interest. While it's ideal to have a local health literacy network, this is often not possible. Instead of (or in addition to) in-person meetings, you might find an online network of health literacy colleagues. I know that I learn a tremendous amount from the more than 500 health and literacy colleagues around the world who subscribe to NIFL-Health listserv—an online health literacy discussion group sponsored by the National Institute for Literacy (http://nifl.gov/lincs).

Your health literacy network can also include those with compatible experiences and interests. Increasingly, communities are building health literacy networks and coalitions with representation from health facilities, literacy programs, libraries, businesses, social service agencies, and the public at large.

Learn from those around you. Health literacy is bigger than any one person, profession, or program. A lot of my knowledge comes from watching and talking to others who face similar, yet not identical, challenges. For example, I learn a lot about communicating with patients from other languages and cultures by watching an English as Second Language (ESL) teacher working with middle school students. And I appreciate the power of pictographs even more when I see how graphic artists convey complex ideas with just a few lines and squiggles. And when patients and family members tell me stories about how hard it is to understand health information, I remember again why I do this work. Just look around you. The world is filled with health literacy zest and pizzazz.

Zest and pizzazz start with knowing why you are passionate about health literacy.

Sources to Learn More

Doak CC, Doak LG, Root JH, 1996. *Teaching Patients with Low Literacy Skills,* 2nd ed. Philadelphia, PA: J.B. Lippincott Company.

Health Literacy Consulting. Available at http://www.healthliteracy.com. Accessed January 29, 2004.

Health Literacy Month. Available at http://www.healthliteracymonth.org. Accessed January 29, 2004.

NIFL-Health (an online discussion group about health literacy sponsored by the National Institute for Literacy). Available at http://www.nifl.gov/lincs. Accessed January 29, 2004.

Osborne H, 2003. "In other words...it's time to get involved in health literacy month," *On Call* magazine, 6(9):16–17. Available at http://www. healthliteracy.com. Accessed January 29, 2004. Information is adapted and reprinted with permission of *On Call* magazine. *On Call* is published by Boston Works, a division of the *Boston Globe.*

_____, 2002a. "In other words...health-literacy partnerships...working together can make a difference," *On Call* magazine, 5(9):16–17. Available at http://www.healthliteracy.com. Accessed January 29, 2004. Information is adapted and reprinted with permission of *On Call* magazine. *On Call* is published by Boston Works, a division of the *Boston Globe*.

_____, 2002b. *Partnering with Patients To Improve Health Outcomes*. Gaithersburg, MD: Aspen Publishers, Inc.

_____, 2001a. "In other words...when you need to know...literacy resources for health professionals," *On Call* magazine, 4(2):34–35. Available at http://www.healthliteracy.com. Accessed January 29, 2004. Information is adapted and reprinted with permission of *On Call* magazine. *On Call* is published by Boston Works, a division of the *Boston Globe*.

_____, 2001b. "In other words...make a difference...be a literacy volunteer," *On Call* magazine, 4(4):38–39. Available at http://www.healthliteracy.com. Accessed January 29, 2004. Information is adapted and reprinted with permission of *On Call* magazine. *On Call* is published by Boston Works, a division of the *Boston Globe*.

_____, 2000a. *Overcoming Communication Barriers in Patient Education*. Gaithersburg, MD: Aspen Publishers, Inc.

_____, 2000b. "In other words...health literacy month...it's time to get involved," *On Call* magazine, 3(9):34–35. Available at http://www.healthliteracy.com. Accessed January 29, 2004. Information is adapted and reprinted with permission of *On Call* magazine. *On Call* is published by Boston Works, a division of the *Boston Globe*.

Eight Ways You Can Improve Health Communication

1. **Know your audience, in general.** Begin by getting familiar with the "average" person in your patient population or intended audience. This means learning about literacy level, language, culture, and age. It also means being sensitive to disability and to emotions which may affect how the average person understands and uses health information.

2. **Tailor communication, in specific.** No one really is "average." After you know where to begin, tailor or adapt your communication to meet the needs of each individual. This may be drawing pictographs for someone who speaks limited English, or teaching just one concept at a time to someone who has trouble concentrating. You can also tailor

communication by offering additional resources for people who want to learn more.

3. **Create a welcoming and supportive environment.** Whether your environment is in a building or somewhere in cyberspace, make sure that it is safe, feels private, and encourages thought and reasoned action. As well, set a tone in which people can comfortably ask questions, disagree, and tell you when they don't understand.

4. **Communicate in whatever ways work.** People learn and communicate in a variety of ways. Beyond just talking or using written materials, consider options like metaphors, objects, and models. Apply the principles of plain language to all forms of communication. This includes using words that people already know, teaching ones they need to learn, and presenting information from the other person's point of view.

5. **Confirm understanding.** Communication is only effective when the other person understands. Confirm what people do and do not know. When there are gaps, rephrase; do not just repeat information. Make sure, as well, that you truly understand what the other person is communicating to you.

6. **Offer ways to learn more.** You needn't communicate everything to everyone all at once. In fact, too much information can lead to confusion. Instead, communicate what people need to know now and provide credible resources to learn more later.

7. **Weigh the ethics of simplicity.** Your role as a health communicator is to translate complex scientific and medical information into words and concepts that patients and families can understand. This is hard to do, especially when information is ambiguous or conflicting. As you decide which information to leave in or omit, consider the implications of these choices.

8. **Collaborate for good communication.** Health literacy and good communication go beyond just one person, profession, or program. Collaborate with your patients, colleagues, and community. Working together, you *can* improve health understanding.

Health Literacy Month

Health Literacy Month, celebrated each October, is a time when health literacy advocates around the world promote the importance of understandable health information. Started in 1999, this month serves as a common focus that hospitals, health centers, literacy programs, libraries, social service agencies, schools, businesses, professional associations, government groups, consumer alliances, and a myriad of other organizations use to draw attention and develop local capacity to address health literacy.

October 1 – 31

Health Literacy Month

Finding
the Right Words
for Better
Health

www.healthliteracymonth.org

There is no right or wrong way to participate in Health Literacy Month. Individuals and organizations can get involved in ways that match their skills, interests, resources, and identified community needs. Some people, for example, talk about health literacy in department meetings and put up Health Literacy Month posters. Others sponsor health literacy workshops or display health literacy information in their local libraries and shopping malls. Some even work with their state governments to officially proclaim October as Health Literacy Month. Large or small, community-based or nationwide, the shared goal of these events is to improve health understanding.

A key component of this initiative is the Health Literacy Month website available at www.healthliteracymonth.org. This site includes FAQ's, articles, posters, links, and other practical resources. It also has a worldwide map where organizations can post ways to help raise health literacy awareness. Health Literacy Month is listed in numerous databases and publications including *Chase's Calendar of Events* (Chicago, IL: Contemporary Books) and the Center for Disease Control's *National Health Observances Calendar*, http://www.healthfinder. gov/library/nho/nho.asp#m10.

Helen Osborne is the founder and director of Health Literacy Month. To learn more, you can contact her by email at Helen@healthliteracy.com. You are also welcome to visit Helen's Health Literacy Consulting website at www.healthliteracy.com.

Health Literacy Month belongs to all of us.

Working together, we CAN make a difference!

About
Helen Osborne

Healthcare and creativity are my life-long interests. When I was young, I thought I needed to choose between these interests and I remember being torn between whether to be a doctor or an artist. Happily, as I got older, I learned that I can combine these interests. In fact, I often do.

As an occupational therapist working in psychiatry, I treated patients who couldn't read, didn't speak English, had limited vision or hearing, or were too sick to communicate. Instead of just talking, I often helped them focus and interact through activities such as drawing or crafts. I used creativity in my administrative work as well. Whether managing a rehabilitation department or chairing committees, I used pictures and diagrams to clarify key points and to help professionals of divergent perspectives come to consensus.

Now, when I lead health literacy workshops, I use hands-on activities like case stories and role-playing scenarios so participants can practice the concepts I teach. As a writer—for the lay public and health professionals alike—I use stories, metaphors, and examples to make key points come alive. Health Literacy Month, which I established, is a creative activity as well. This annual event began as my middle-of-the night notion and has grown to be a successful worldwide initiative. And my business, Health Literacy Consulting, exists and thrives because I continually look for new and creative ways to communicate—in person, in print, and online.

Health Literacy From A to Z: Practical Ways to Communicate Your Health Message is yet another creative outlet—one that provides me with an opportunity to encourage you to call on your creative talents.

Healthcare and creativity work well together. Indeed, this combination is the key to communicating in ways that people can truly understand.

Thank you for joining me in this effort.

~Helen

Helen Osborne, MEd OTR/L
President, Health Literacy Consulting

****

To learn more about my work in health literacy, please visit the Health Literacy Consulting website at www.healthliteracy.com.

To learn more about Health Literacy Month, please go to www.healthliteracymonth.org.

You are also welcome to contact me by email at Helen@ healthliteracy.com

Index